Queensland Islands

A TRAVEL AND HOLIDAY GUIDE

David Stranger, a film-maker and teacher, was born in Melbourne in 1951. While in his early twenties he drove around Australia, pausing in the West to work as a surveyor's assistant in the Pilbara. In 1975 he visited the USA, where he studied film production at the Berkely Film Institute. He has made a number of short films, one of which, *Bad Rocks*, was nominated for an Australian Film Institute award in 1988. David Stranger currently teaches in secondary schools in central Victoria.

Queensland Islands

A TRAVEL AND HOLIDAY GUIDE

David Stranger

Houghton Mifflin Australia

Acknowledgements

I would like to thank those people who gave me information about the islands that I could have not found out for myself: to Marcus Arthur for his help on the islands off Cape York, to Harold Marshall for his help with Fraser Island and Sue and Rodger Taylor for their assistance with Bedarra Island.

Thanks to Big Cat Cruises, Cairns, South Mission Beach Water-taxi, Cairns Backpackers Inn and Backpackers Paddington for making life easier for an impoverished traveller.

The Division of Conservation, Parks and Wildlife and the John Oxley Library, Brisbane, were a great help with camping and historical information.

And finally, thanks to Wendy Hannis for the typing, Ilze Osenieks for the word processing, James Stranger for the photocopying, Stan Wilcox for the proofreading, John Brownlie for getting me started and Monica Ericson for... just being Monica Ericson.

Houghton Mifflin Australia Pty Ltd
PO Box 289, Ferntree Gully, Victoria 3156
112 Lewis Rd, Knoxfield, Victoria 3180, Australia
First Published 1989

National Library of Australia
Cataloguing-in-Publication entry:

Stranger, David.
Queensland Islands: A Travel and holioday guide

Includes index.
ISBN 0 86770 103 X.

1. Islands — Queensland — Description and travel — Guide-books. 2. Tourist camps, hostels, etc. — Queensland — Guide-books. 3. Queensland — Description and travel — 1976 - — Guide-books. I. Title.

919 . 430463

Edited by Margaret Jones
Designed by J.Harvey Hapi
Produced by Mitchell Publishing
Typeset in Garamond by Mitchell Publishing
Printed by Australian Print Group, Maryborough, Victoria

Contents

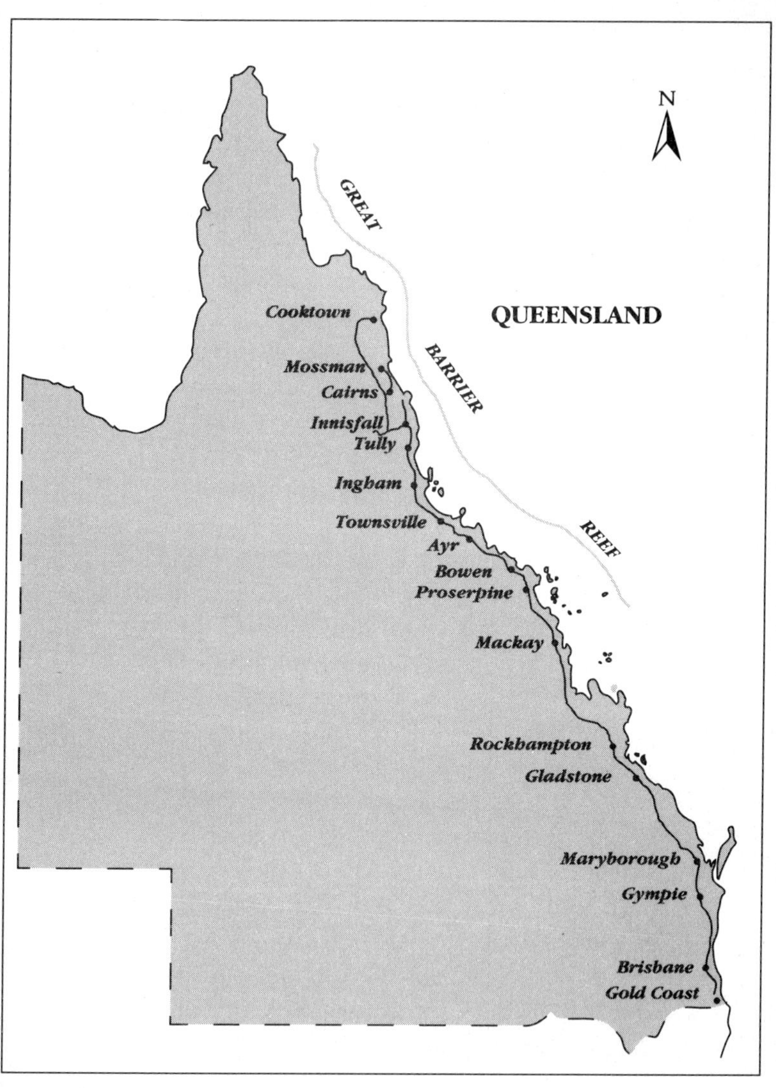
N
GREAT
BARRIER
REEF
QUEENSLAND
Cooktown
Mossman
Cairns
Innisfail
Tully
Ingham
Townsville
Ayr
Bowen
Proserpine
Mackay
Rockhampton
Gladstone
Maryborough
Gympie
Brisbane
Gold Coast

Introduction

Queensland has more than 1200 islands stretching along its 3400 km coastline.

This book is intended as a basic travel guide to those islands of Queensland that are relatively easy to reach and stay on.

Islands with resorts, numbering about 20, are listed and I have included as much information as I have been able to gather on islands suitable for camping. Prices quoted were correct at the time of writing but should be checked.

The book caters mostly for the backpacker or traveller who depends on land transport and launch services to move around. It does not contain detailed boating information as there are a number of books available on this subject. Several are listed in the bibliography.

Apart from Thursday, Magnetic, Curtis, Bribie and North and South Stradbroke Islands, which have many private blocks of land, there are more than 100 islands owned privately under freehold title and more than 250 under lease. Ansett, Australian Airlines and Hamilton Island's Keith Williams are the three biggest owners and leaseholders.

Over 200 islands are national parks and permits are needed to stay there. A new permit system for camping in Queensland's national parks was introduced in 1988. Parks have been divided into three fee categories:

category A: $7 per site per night
category B: $5 per site per night
category C: $2 per person per night or
$5 maximum for six people

There is a limit of six people per site. Coupons are the preferred method of payment although cash is accepted. Coupons are available from all offices of the Division of Conservation, Parks and Wildlife (DCPW). It is suggested that campers intending to be away from civilization for some time take an additional three meals (one a day for three days) and 15 litres of water (five litres per day for three days) in the event of being stranded. The inclusion of a first-aid kit is also advisable.

Many of the resorts lease small areas of land on national park islands. The remainder of the islands are vacant crown land, many of them too inaccessible or tiny to bother about, local council reserves, Aboriginal reserves and the odd lighthouse reserve.

The islands became popular tourist destinations with the development of air travel after World War II. One of the greatest drawcards was the Great Barrier Reef. The reef, now largely protected as a marine park under the Great Barrier Reef Marine Park Authority, stretches from the small coral cay of Lady Elliot Island off Bundaberg to Papua New Guinea, a distance of more than 2000 km.

The reefs, for there are many reefs within the Great Barrier Reef, are formed by coral. Coral can grow as free-standing clumps well out to sea (platform and wall reefs) or, just as often, off the mainland coast or around islands closer to shore (fringing reefs). Coral is made by tiny animals, relatives of the jellyfish and sea anemones. They absorb calcium and oxygen from sea water to form lime which they use to house themselves. When the coral polyp dies, hard limestone is left and another coral polyp builds on top of it, thus creating a 'growing' reef. But because the polyp can't exist out of water for very long, reefs do not grow further than low-tide level. Neither can they survive in water too deep because they need sunlight for algae that live within their tissue.

Many of the resort islands have launch services to the Outer Reef and some of these are listed in the book. Launches used are usually large-capacity, motorized catamarans travelling at speeds up to 30 knots. A danger with the increasing number of high-speed boats being used as transfer craft is the number of sea creatures such as dugong and turtles that are injured and killed. Development in Queensland needs some restraint.

Be mindful of the sensitive island and reef environment and treat it with respect. It's the only one we've got.

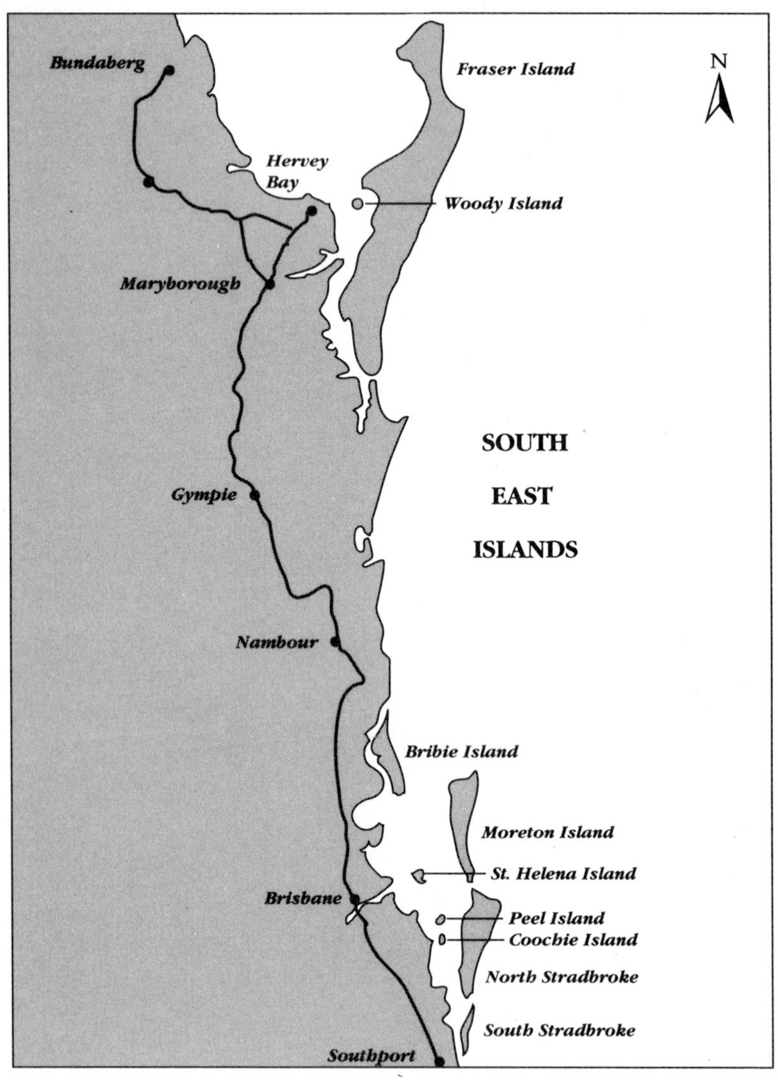
Bundaberg
Fraser Island
N
Hervey
Bay
Woody Island
Maryborough
SOUTH
EAST
ISLANDS
Gympie
Nambour
Bribie Island
Moreton Island
St. Helena Island
Brisbane
Peel Island
Coochie Island
North Stradbroke
South Stradbroke
Southport

The South East Islands

The South East Islands are mostly sand islands stretching along the coast from South Stradbroke near the Gold Coast to the biggest sand deposit of them all, Fraser Island.

The islands are formed by silt washed down in mainland rivers and then carried northwards by sea currents. They are characterized by long stretches of sandy beaches and well-established vegetation.

Brisbane, the capital city of Queensland, is the main centre in the region.

South Stradbroke Island

- **Resort**
- **Campground**
- **Bush camping**
- **Water**
- **Toilets**
- **Picnic area**
- **Fireplace**
- **Phone**
- **Ranger staff**
- **Walking tracks**

South Stradbroke is a long, sandy island, much like its next-door neighbour North Stradbroke. The two islands were once connected but a cyclone in 1896 caused them to split in two and a gap to be formed. This is known as Jumpinpin or simply 'The Pin'.

South Stradbroke is 20 km long but only about 2 km across at its widest point. It's flat and mostly forested. It has one small resort on the calm waters of its western side. Tipplers, as the resort is known, is popular with boaties and day-trippers from the Gold Coast and can be quite crowded during the day.

The only other settlements are at Couran and Currigee. They both consist of privately owned blocks.

There were plans put forward by the Hooker-Rex company in the 1950s to turn the island into a huge Florida-style development complete with hotels, heliports and a hospital. Ironically, the idea was scrapped when sand-mining companies opposed the development because they would have had to surrender their leases.

Fortunately, the local shire and the state government have seen the value of the area as a recreation and conservation zone and have begun declaring some of the nearby islands environmental parks. The area, which stretches from Paradise Point at the northern tip of the Gold Coast to past the southern extremity of North Stradbroke, is a major fish breeding estuary with mudflats, mangroves, sandbars and islands. Some of the larger islands, such as Woogoompah, have large stands of eucalypt while others, like Eden Island, are covered in salt marsh.

Tipplers resort has cruises out to the Jumpinpin bar for $5. It also hires out small boats, catamarans and jet skis.

The resort is not blessed with natural attributes. Its terrain is rather flat and uninteresting, the beach is narrow and the water murky. It has a bistro and restaurant but the bistro food is pretty ordinary, although reasonably priced. There is no cooking allowed at the resort if you happen to be a guest, but a takeaway food shop gives everyone a bit more choice.

Tipplers has a bar, of course, and the shop sells boat fuel.

ACCESS

The main means of access to the island is Tipplers resort's water taxi, *Tipplers Islander Express*. It leaves from the C2 berth at Runaway Bay marina in Bayview Street, Runaway Bay, a few kilometres north of Southport.

A seaplane operates from Marina Mirage on the Gold Coast or from South Brisbane. Ring Tipplers, or Sea-Air on 075 372279, for details.

There are numerous daytripper launches that run from the Gold Coast and stop at Tipplers for lunch. Ring Tipplers for details.

ACCOMMODATION

The resort has attractive Fijian-style octagonal units. Each unit (one or two bedrooms) has amenities such as shower, toilet, refrigerator and colour TV. In the low season they cost $22.50 per person per night on a twin-share basis or $40 per night for sole use. That's for accommodation only, but there's full board as well.

Tipplers can be contacted on 075 573311 or toll-free on 008 074125.

CAMPING

There is a campground just south of the resort run by the Albert Shire Council. It's within easy walking distance of the resort, which has a restaurant, bistro, bar and shop.

The campground has a picnic area and shower and toilet block. The council ranger lives here. It is possible to camp on other parts of the island for $4 a night. Check with the ranger.

Campers are welcome to use the resort shop and other eating areas but not facilities such as the pool or tennis court.

WALKING TRACKS

There are several tracks that span out from the resort. They are all vehicular tracks but cars are banned on the island so a walker can walk in peace.

The best walk is probably the one to the ocean beach. It starts behind Tipplers resort and cuts straight across the island to the superb 14 km white sandy beach on the other side. It's a great place to escape to from the hustle and bustle of the resort. It's an easy 15-minute stroll.

There are two more tracks that run out from the resort, one heading north and the other south. Both of them hug the foreshore. The southern track passes through the Albert Shire campground and various private boat-club leases. The north track is less crowded and runs through a mixed species forest of melaleucas, banksias, eucalypts, cypress pines and mangroves, all at the water's edge.

The manager informs me that both of these tracks wind back to a middle road that spines the island from end to end.

CLOSEST DCPW OFFICE

Burleigh Heads
Gold Coast Highway
Burleigh Heads
Queensland 4220
075 353032

NEAREST HELP

A helicopter can be called on in an emergency to take people to Southport, or Tipplers have basic first-aid facilities.

North Stradbroke Island

Coochie Mudlo Island & Peel Island

- **Resort**
- **Campground**
- **Bush camping**
- **Water**
- **Toilets**
- **Picnic area**
- **Fireplace**
- **Phone**
- **Walking tracks**
- **Suitable for disabled**

North Stradbroke is the closest large island to Brisbane. It is only 30 km from Brisbane and 13 km off the coast. This means that there's easy access to beaches with good swimming, fishing and surfing on the one hand, but widespread exploitation by sand-mining and forestry industries on the other. In 1973, 90 percent of the island was leased for sand-mining operations.

North Stradbroke, like its neighbours South Stradbroke and Moreton Islands, is a sand island that has been formed from silt washed down from rivers in northern New South Wales. It stretches for 40 km and is 10 km at its widest point. **Main Beach**, the ocean beach on the eastern side, is 35 km long and is ideal for foreshore camping.

The island has a full-time population of over 3000 and most of the public roads are sealed but, be warned, there's only one bank, an ANZ.

Most people get the car ferry across to **Dunwich**, on the western side of the island. Established as a military barracks and a convict settlement, the town has the island's only garage, and boat facilities are available at the Dunwich Yacht Club. The road to the ocean beach, Blue Lake and Brown Lake starts at Dunwich as does the road to Point Lookout and Amity Point.

Brown Lake can be reached by car and has a picnic area with barbecue and toilets.

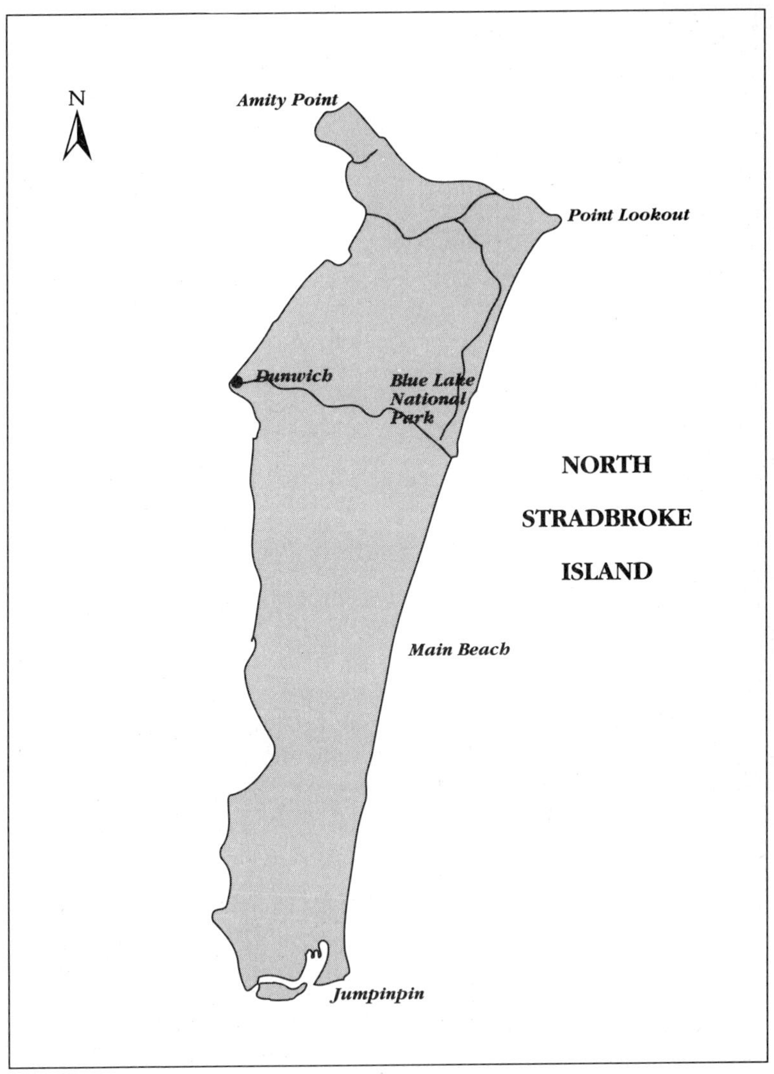
N
Amity Point
Point Lookout
Dunwich
Blue Lake
National
Park
NORTH
STRADBROKE
ISLAND
Main Beach
Jumpinpin

Blue Lake is accessible only by four-wheel drive or foot. See Walking Tracks for more details.

Point Lookout is the most attractive spot on the island. It has secluded beaches, headlands, walking tracks, the only hotel and the only backpacker hostel. It's from Point Lookout that humpback whales can be seen on their way up to Hervey Bay to have their young. That's between May and July. From August to October they make the return journey to Antarctica.

See the Anchorage Village resort for the hire of a four-wheel drive or to get a taxi.

Point Lookout is also known for its lentilburgers, available at the Point Lookout kiosk.

Amity Point started as a pilot station for ships tackling the South Passage, the stretch of water that divides North Stradbroke from Moreton Island. After many a shipwreck, the passage was closed to ships. There are various smaller islands between North Stradbroke and the mainland.

Coochie Mudlo Island

Coochie Mudlo Island is only a few kilometres from the mainland coast. A ferry runs from Victoria Point. It takes cars only (with their passengers) and takes 10 minutes to get across. Ring 07 2077287 for details.

The Bayside bus service runs between the city and Victoria Point. Their number in Manly is 07 3968055.

A bus service operates on the island and moke and boat hire is available.

Coochie Mudlo is a mere 130 hectares, so circumnavigating it on foot is quite possible. The island has beaches, a store and kiosk, restaurant, tea rooms, a golf course and tennis court. People live on this island and commute to work on the mainland. There are holiday houses for rent or you can try Coochie-Ville on 07 2077521 for units.

The island is popular with day-trippers and picnickers, and very popular during school holidays.

Peel Island

Peel Island used to be used as a base to extract oil fromthe dugong or sea-cow. It is only accessible by private boat, and there is a jetty and anchorage in the bay on the north side. Consisting mostly of mangroves, mudflats and sandbanks, it is a popular fishing spot. Peel Island is the one seen from the ferry on the approach to Dunwich.

ACCESS

North Stradbroke is well serviced by a variety of transport. If you are going by car, there's a ferry service from Cleveland at the end of Middle Street. It goes across up to 12 times a day and costs $48 return for a car or $4 if you're just taking yourself across. Ring 07 2862666 to confirm times and to book. The trip takes about an hour.

There's another car ferry from Redland

Bay. It arrives at Dunwich on North Stradbroke, as does the ferry from Cleveland. It runs five times a day. Ring 07 3582122 for details.

The Stradbroke Island bus service goes all the way to Point Lookout, via Cleveland. It leaves from Brisbane City Council bus stop No.1 at the Transit Centre at 2.15 p.m. Monday to Friday and arrives at Point Lookout at 5 p.m. It leaves at 7.45 a.m. on Saturday and Sunday. Their number is 07 2871275. It costs $7.75 one-way.

The Bayside bus service leaves the Hoyts Centre in Elizabeth Street for Cleveland regularly. The cost is $2.70. Two water-taxi services take only 20 minutes to make the trip. One is operated by Stradbroke Ferries, who run the car ferry from Cleveland and charge $5 return, and the other by Island Taxi Service (07 2861964), who charge $9 return.

ACCOMMODATION

The only backpacker accommodation at present is the **Point Lookout Hostel** on East Coast Road. This 24-bed hostel has a spacious living area underneath bunkrooms, some of which have their own bathroom and kitchen. It's good value for $10 and Drew Henderson makes a good host.

Their number is 075 498279. The Brisbane bus runs right past the door.

The main resort on North Stradbroke is

Anchorage Village, also on East Coast Road in Point Lookout but a bit further back towards Dunwich.

For two adults to share a room in low season for a week, the resort charges $490 for its Islander units, $560 for the Beachcomber rooms and $770 for the top-of-the-range Penthouse suites. Their phone number is 075 498266 or toll-free 008 077008.

Anchorage Village boasts a pool with an underwater stereo — surely a unique achievement!

CAMPING

There are camping areas with facilities at **Point Lookout, Dunwich** and **Amity**. The Redland Shire Council Reserve is at Point Lookout, 075 498192.

Bush camping is okay on **Main Beach** from the causeway all the way to the Jumpinpin Bar, as well as on **Flinders Beach** on the north side of the island from 3 km west of Adder Rock. Unless you have a four-wheel drive Flinders Beach is the more accessible of the two.

Camping is not permitted around the lakes.

WALKING TRACKS

Blue Lake is a small national park close to Main Beach on the eastern side of the island. It is reached by taking Tazi Road across the island from Dunwich. This road ends at the causeway across Eighteen Mile Swamp to Main Beach. The turnoff to Blue Lake is clearly signposted.

It is possible to drive to the lake in a four-wheel drive vehicle but most people have to walk from the car park, 3 km from the lake. There is a walking track along the eastern edge of the lake.

The lake is a good swimming spot, and toilets, picnic areas and barbecues are provided. Called a 'water table window lake', it sits on and below the water table of the island. It's about a 10 km drive from Dunwich.

Point Lookout headland is another good area to walk.

CLOSEST DCPW OFFICE

Southern Regional Centre
PO Box 42
Kenmore
Queensland 4069
07 2020212

NEAREST HELP

The hospital at Dunwich.

St Helena

- **National Park**
- **Water**
- **Toilets**
- **Picnic area**
- **Phone**
- **Ranger staff**
- **Walking tracks**
- **Suitable for disabled**

St Helena is a unique Queensland island. Situated in Moreton Bay near the Brisbane River mouth, it is steeped in colonial history.

Originally intended as a quarantine station, it was converted into a high-security prison in 1867 due to overcrowding in Brisbane jails. It remained a prison for 65 years. In this time, prison labour was used for all building construction, farming and cooking. They worked a 12-hour day.

Most of the island was declared a national park in 1979 after operating as a private dairy farm since 1932. The colorful Chas Carroll was the last owner. He liked to spend five days a week there looking after his cattle, leaving his family in Brisbane.

Its small size of 166 hectares makes for a leisurely stroll around its many ruins and its closeness to Brisbane makes it a good day trip. There is no camping or accommodation on the island. No food is available so lunch should be taken, or ordered with St Helena Ferries (see under Access).

St Helena doesn't have good beaches but it is something of a bird sanctuary with over 70 species sighted. There are no feral cats on the island.

Known as the 'Hellhole of the Pacific' in its days as a prison for the hardest criminals, it was Queensland's Port Arthur. There were 50 escape attempts in its history — not surprising given the treatment that prisoners

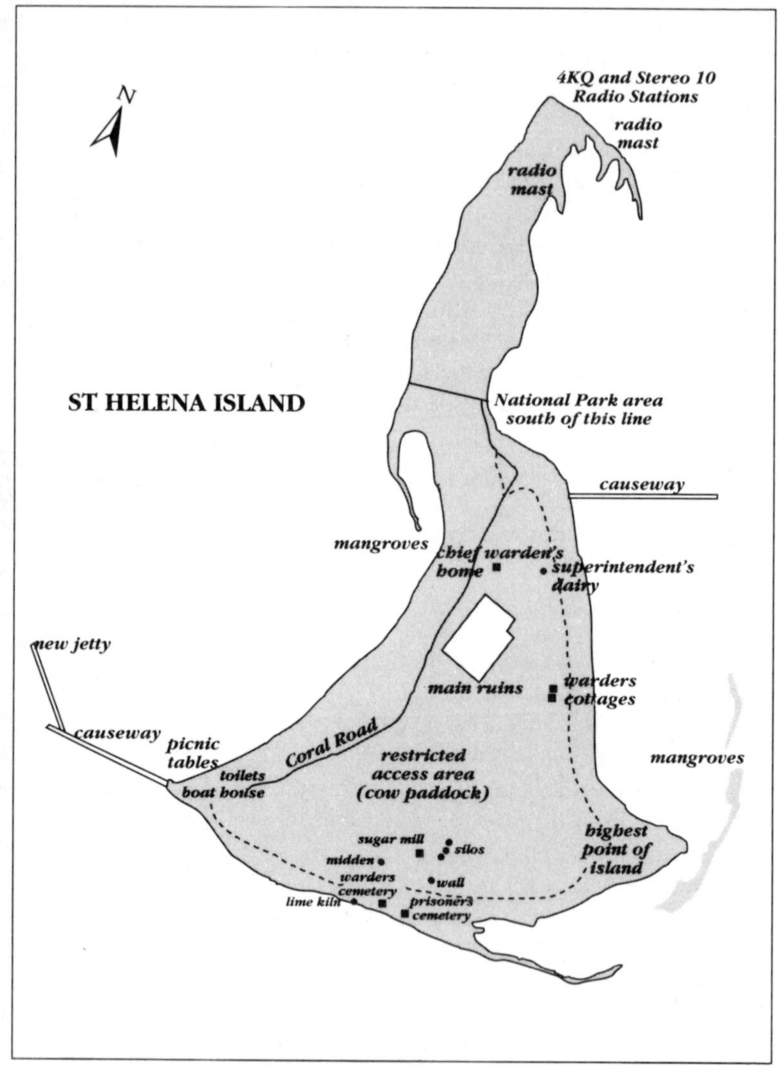

N
4KQ and Stereo 10
Radio Stations
radio
mast
radio
mast
ST HELENA ISLAND
National Park area
south of this line
causeway
mangroves
chief warden's
home
superintendent's
dairy
new jetty
main ruins
warders
cottages
causeway
picnic
tables
toilets
boat house
Coral Road
restricted
access area
(cow paddock)
mangroves
highest
point of
island
sugar mill
silos
midden
warders
cemetery
wall
lime kiln
prisoners
cemetery

received. Henry Wheeler got seven days in solitary confinement for singing: his ration was about 680g of bread and water a day.

Although the island's natural isolation made escape difficult, the administration made it that much harder by flushing the offal of slaughtered cattle, sheep and pigs out into the bay in order to attract sharks.

Only one escapee was never recaptured. He was Charles Leslie, a notorious gunman, who was picked up on the foreshore by friends in a motor boat in 1924. Many of the prisoners took to suicide as their last means of escape.

The lush green tranquility of St Helena today belies any notion of having been a 'Hellhole'. It is a fascinating excursion into history and should not be missed.

ACCESS

Manly is the jumping-off point for St Helena Island. This bayside suburb of Brisbane is reached by car (take a street directory as signs are scarce), by Queensland Railways train or Bayside bus.

Graham Carter's catamaran leaves from the northern side of the jetty at the end of Cardigan Parade in Manly. School groups use the service on weekdays. Graham will take individuals as well on these days but you should ring St Helena Ferries first on 07 3933726 to make a reservation. Fares include a guided tour, and a light lunch can be provided on request.

The island sits about 8 km out to sea, and the trip across takes 25 minutes.

WALKING TRACKS

As St Helena is a small island with a gentle slope, walking is easy over most of it. There are restricted access areas in the main ruins area, the fenced-off cow paddock and the northern tip of the island. Radio stations 4KQ and Stereo 10 have their transmission towers here.

A good, easy walk runs from the jetty and up the hill to the main ruins. Further up the rise to the north-east are sweeping views across to Moreton and North Stradbroke Islands. From here head south by hugging the eastern hill edge, around the cow paddock and past the sugar mill and prisoner cemetery and back to the jetty. Allow at least one hour for this walk. The grade is easy.

CLOSEST DCPW OFFICE

St Helena Office
PO Box 66
Manly
Queensland 4179
07 3965113

NEAREST HELP

Manly

Moreton Island

- **National Park (categories B and C)**
- **Resort**
- **Campground**
- **Bush camping**
- **Water**
- **Toilets**
- **Phone**
- **Ranger staff**
- **Suitable for disabled**

Moreton Island is a large sand island in Moreton Bay, similar in shape and size to its neighbour to the south, North Stradbroke Island. But fortunately for Moreton, mining has not been as extensive nor its impact as noticeable. After public opposition to state government plans to allow sand-mining on 60 percent of the land, 89 percent of the island is now national park.

Situated about 40 km north-east of Brisbane, the island stretches for 38km and is 9 km at its widest point. It's noted for its sandy beaches which surround the island, and freshwater lakes. **Blue Lagoon** and **Honeyeater Lake**, on the eastern side, are easily accessible from the road.

The land is covered in heathlands, swamps and forests of banksias, cypress, paperbarks, bloodwoods and scribbly gums. There are pockets of grasstrees and foxtail ferns, and she-oak and brushbox are seen in the north and east respectively.

Feral pigs, goats and horses populate the island but not, as yet, the cane toad, so prolific in other areas of Queensland.

Moreton Island has three small towns, **Bulwer, Kooringal and Cowan Cowan**. It has one resort at **Tangalooma.**

Bulwer was the first European settlement, established in 1848 when the Amity Point pilot station was moved there after the South Passage was closed to shipping. Bulwer

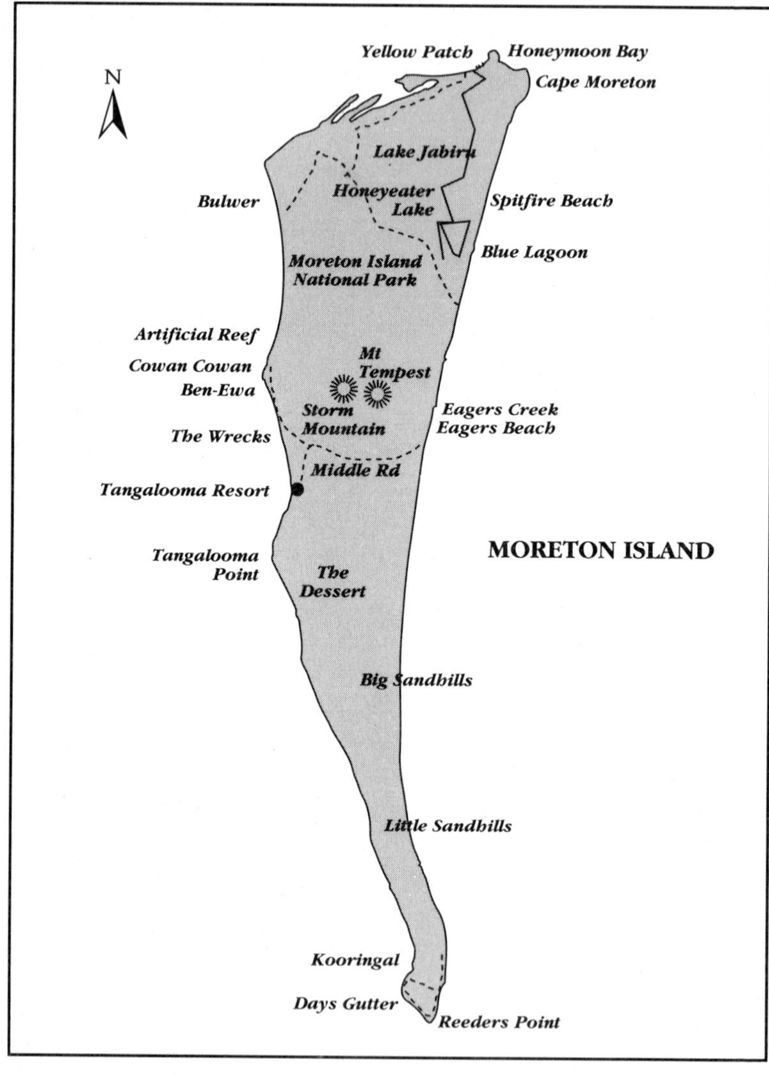
Yellow Patch
Honeymoon Bay
N
Cape Moreton
Lake Jabiru
Honeyeater Lake
Bulwer
Spitfire Beach
Blue Lagoon
Moreton Island National Park
Artificial Reef
Mt Tempest
Cowan Cowan
Ben-Ewa
Storm Mountain
Eagers Creek
Eagers Beach
The Wrecks
Middle Rd
Tangalooma Resort
MORETON ISLAND
Tangalooma Point
The Dessert
Big Sandhills
Little Sandhills
Kooringal
Days Gutter
Reeders Point

today has the only garage on the island (075 481335) and is the place to go to hire camping equipment or bikes (075 482661). There is also a shop here.

Kooringal has a shop as well and one of two public phones; the other one is at Tangalooma.

Four-wheel drives can be hired at Kooringal (075 497170) or Bulwer (075 482202). Fuel is available at the Bulwer garage or the Kooringal shop. All roads are unsealed on Moreton Island and a four-wheel drive is recommended.

Cowan Cowan was established as a defence post after World War I. Some of the old Army buildings are now home to the Moreton Bay Boat Club and its rescue service (see under Nearest Help).

An interesting feature just north of Cowan Cowan is the artificial **Curtin Reef**, now home of myriad forms of marine life. Dumped here are tugboats, whaling chasers, barges, cars, 5000 truck and car tyres and even an old Brisbane tram. Spearfishing is banned on the bay side of the island.

South of here, in between Cowan Cowan and Tangalooma resort, is another graveyard of old boats called **The Wrecks**. If you have the slightest interest in marine history or an eye for the bizarre, a visit to The Wrecks is a must. The boats were sunk here to create a safe anchorage for other boats.

Ben-Ewa camping area is near here (see

under Camping) and 2 km south is **Tangalooma** (for more about the resort, see Accommodation). Campers are permitted into the resort during the day and at evenings if 'clean and well-behaved', in the words of the manager. If in doubt, ask at reception.

More information is available about Moreton Island in the Sunmap and the DCPW sheet, available at the national parks office situated between The Wrecks and Ben-Ewa campground.

ACCESS

A passenger service is supplied by Tangalooma resort to guests and day-trippers alike, on the *Tangalooma Flyer.* It leaves Holt Street, in Pinkenba, at 9.30 a.m. Tuesday to Friday and 9.00 a.m. Saturday and Sunday. It costs $30 return for guests and $36 for day-trippers (includes lunch). The journey takes one and a quarter hours.

Ring the resort on 07 2686333 for more details.

The *Moreton Venture* car ferry runs from White Island to Kooringal and Tangalooma. Telephone 07 8951000.

A light-plane service is available at the General Aviation Terminal, Light Aircraft Section, at Eagle Farm Airport, Brisbane, for around $70 return. The trip takes a quick 15 minutes and lands at either of two airstrips on the island, at Kooringal or Cowan Cowan.

ACCOMMODATION

Moreton Island has one resort at **Tangalooma**. It started life as a whaling station in the 1950s but was closed in 1962 after whales were severely reduced in numbers and the world price of whale oil fell. The original flensing deck is now the floor of the administration block of the resort.

Tangalooma boasts unlimited fresh water, child-care facilities, sandy beaches, cool sea breezes, the absence of box jelly-fish, and a well-looked after native garden. However, because of its size and its popularity as a day-visitor destination, it can get pretty busy, particularly on weekends.

The resort has units of one or two bedrooms. With two adults sharing in low season for a week Standard rooms cost $595, Beachcomber rooms $665, Driftwood rooms $735 and Suites $805.

Contact
Tangalooma Resort
PO Box 1102
Eagle Farm
Queensland 4007
07 2686333

Other unit accommodation is available at **Kooringal**. Ring 075 497170.

CAMPING

Camping areas with water, toilets and cold

showers are at Blue Lagoon and Eagers Creek on the ocean side of the island and Ben-Ewa and The Wrecks on the bay side.

Beach camping draws a category B fee and bush camping a category C fee. Moreton will be the first island to be declared under the Recreation Area Management Act, and some changes in fee structure may take place. See the Ranger at Ben-Ewa for more information. His number is 075 482710.

CLOSEST DCPW OFFICE

The island has a DCPW office about 3 km north of the resort near Ben-Ewa camping reserve.

The address is:

The Ranger
DCPW
c/o Tangalooma Resort
Moreton Island
Queensland 4025
075 482710

NEAREST HELP

There is a resident doctor at Tangalooma resort.

Moreton Bay Boat Club operates a rescue service. Their call sign is VJ 4 MT.

Bribie Island

Bribie Island, like Magnetic Island to the north, is one of the few islands along the coast that could be called residential. Being only a 45 minute drive from Brisbane, it's a popular family destination during holiday periods and probably has as many retirement villages to the hectare as the Gold Coast.

A flat, featureless sand island of Moreton Bay, its main attraction seems to be the ocean beach on its eastern side. Although camping is not permitted on the beach, it's possible to drive along it if you have a permit from the Caboolture Shire Council.

Only the southern end of the island is settled, with the suburb of Woorim on the ocean beach and Bongaree and Bellara on the mainland side. There's safe swimming at Bongaree but the beach is weedy.

A 2000-hectare national park has been declared on the western side of the island. There is a camping area at **Mission Point** across from Donnybrook on the mainland, with boat access only. An environmental park is to be declared on the eastern ocean side.

Boats may be hired from the Spinnaker Sound marina on the mainland side of the bridge to the island, and cars from the BP service station in Bongaree.

- **National Park (category C)**
- **Water**
- **Toilets**
- **Picnic area**
- **Fireplace**
- **Phone**
- **Suitable for disabled**

ACCESS
Bribie Island is connected to the mainland by a bridge. The turn-off to the island is 44 km north of Brisbane on the Bruce Highway.

ACCOMMODATION
Bribie Island, being a popular family holiday place, has a number of caravan parks and motels. Consult the local telephone directory.

CLOSEST DCPW OFFICE
Glass House Mountains Office
Roys Road
Beerwah
Queensland 4519
071 946630

Bongaree jetty, Bribie Island.

Fraser Island

Woody Island and Little Woody Island

- National Park
- Resort
- Campground
- Bush camping
- Water
- Toilets
- Picnic area
- Fireplace
- Phone
- Ranger staff
- Walking tracks
- Suitable for disabled

You've probably heard that **Fraser Island** is the largest sand island in the world. But you might not have heard that it's the biggest island off the Australian coast next to Tasmania or that the size of Fraser is roughly half that of Belgium. Perhaps a good slogan would be 'Get Lost on Fraser Island'.

A Hervey Bay woman once remarked 'God created the world in six days and on the seventh, Fraser Island.' This is a slight exaggeration. The island has a bad litter problem and biting insects, particularly march flies can drive people mad in summer. It is, however, a stunning natural museum of closed forests, crystal-clear creeks with bottoms of pure white sand, clear freshwater lakes and pounding surf beaches.

But how do you get around such a large area? Most people prefer to hire a four-wheel drive if they don't already own one. The sandy inland tracks and the beaches mean that a four-wheel drive is a must. They can be hired in Brisbane, Noosa Heads, Rainbow Beach or Hervey Bay. Expect to pay $75 a day for a minimum of two days for the vehicle, around $25 return for the barge and $15 for a permit. There is no garage on Fraser, but minor repairs can be done at Happy Valley and Eurong.

Permits are needed for vehicles and camping. The main office for permits is at Rainbow Beach (see under Closest DCPW

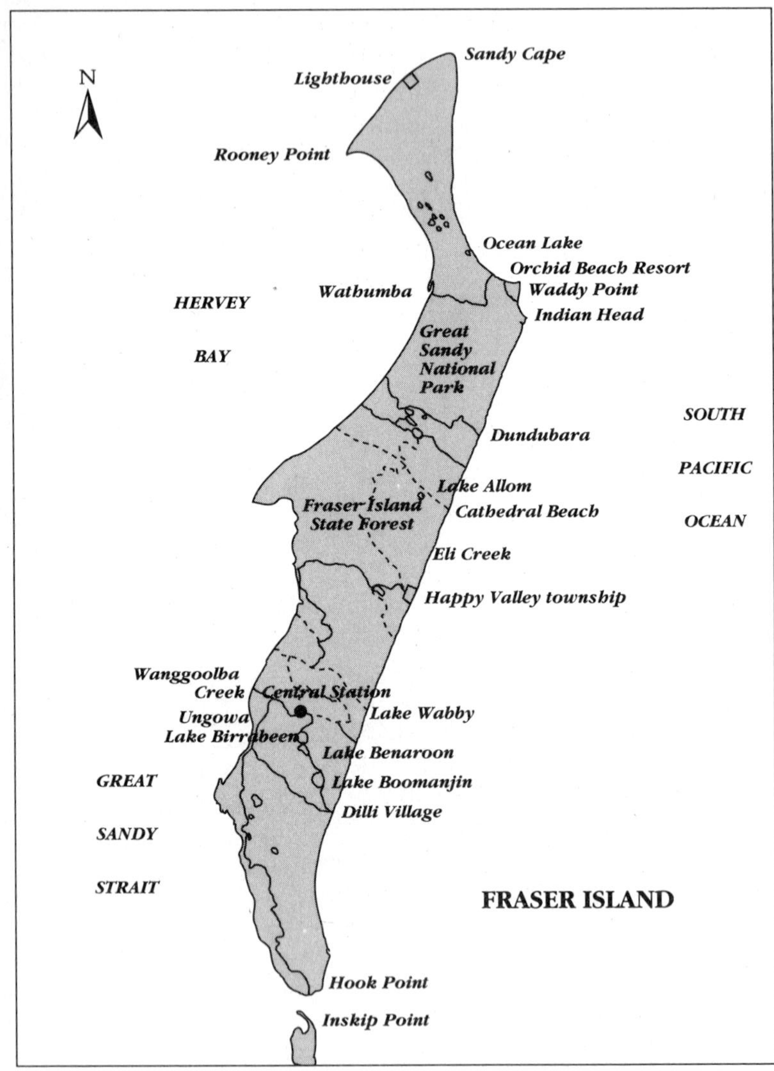

N
Sandy Cape
Lighthouse
Rooney Point
Ocean Lake
Orchid Beach Resort
Waddy Point
Indian Head
Wathumba
HERVEY
BAY
Great
Sandy
National
Park
SOUTH
PACIFIC
OCEAN
Dundubara
Lake Allom
Cathedral Beach
Fraser Island
State Forest
Eli Creek
Happy Valley township
Wanggoolba
Creek
Central Station
Ungowa
Lake Birrabeen
Lake Wabby
Lake Benaroon
Lake Boomanjin
Dilli Village
GREAT
SANDY
STRAIT
FRASER ISLAND
Hook Point
Inskip Point

Office) but they are also available at DCPW offices in Brisbane, Gympie and Maryborough and Department of Forestry offices in Brisbane, Bundaberg, Gympie and Maryborough. The closest office is: Hervey Bay City Council, 10 Bideford Street, Torquay Queensland 4655, 071 251855

Pre-booking is preferred. All mail should be addressed to the Fraser Island Recreation Board c/o the above offices.

Hitchhiking is possible, particularly on the ocean beach where most of the traffic is.

The national park on Fraser Island was established in 1971, the year that sand-mining commenced, strangely enough. Sand-mining was stopped by the federal government in 1976 after one of the biggest conservation campaigns in Australia's history. The Great Sandy National Park only takes in the top third of the island. The remainder, apart from some private land, is state forest or crown land. All of the small pockets of rainforest and other substantial forests are contained within the state forest and are still logged today for their valuable timber.

Timber-getting started in 1863, when the most sought-after tree was white beech which has since been cut out. A timber company from Maryborough — Wilson, Hart and Co.— began hauling logs out of the bush with a steam tram and floating them across to the mainland. In 1883 one of Australia's first tree nurseries was established using the indigenous kauri pine. An original stand of kauri pine has been kept at Yidney Scrub near **Happy Valley**.

Central Station was the hub of the timber industry between 1918 and 1960. Today, **Ungowa** is the headquarters of forestry operations. The majestic satinay and brushbox in the high central ridges and surrounding stands of blackbutt, are the main trees cut today. Satinay is renowned for its resistance to marine borers and was the chosen timber for lining the Suez canal in the 1920s. There is a stand of satinay left in Pile Valley near Central Station. The remaining forests of Fraser Island are chiefly uncommercial areas of scribbly gum, bloodwood or cypress.

There is no shortage of fresh water on Fraser Island. Generally speaking, the major creeks flow to the west coast and springs feed the east. One exception is the fast-flowing Eli Creek on the east coast.

The dingo seen on the island is the purest strain in eastern Australia, as the island's isolation has prevented interbreeding with other dogs. They can be very friendly around campfires, particularly if the scent of barbecued meat is wafting into the bush. There are lots of brumbies too.

Sunmap produce a good map of Fraser and the Fraser Island Recreation Board brochure, *Fraser Island Guide*, gives a list of facilities at camping areas.

Woody Island

Woody Island, between Fraser and the mainland, is a 700-hectare national park island with a camping area at the northern end of the eastern side. This is the only place to bring a boat in. The camping area has tables and fireplaces but no water. There are no restrictions on numbers of campers. The island, used mostly for day visits, is covered in dry sclerophyll woodland and wild goats. There are a few small beaches but no walking tracks. Category C camping.

Little Woody Island

Little Woody Island is another national park where camping is allowed. There is no designated area and no water. Permits from Maryborough DCPW.

ACCESS

Most people go to Fraser Island on a ferry or one of the many day tours. Aircraft are another option.

Vehicle barges run from Inskip Point, near Rainbow Beach, to the southern end of the island. Two barges operate and their telephone numbers are 071 863120 and 071 279122. As well, a barge leaves from River Heads, south of Urangan. The fare is $10 return for passengers and $25 return for vehicles. Their phone number is 071 241900.

There are plenty of day tours to choose from leaving from Hervey Bay.

The *Fraser Flyer* takes you to the western side of the island and four-wheel drive buses then run across to the ocean side at Happy Valley. Their number is 071 251655.

Top Tours concentrate on the northern national park end of the island. Ring them on 071 282577.

The Islander stays in the central area and misses the ocean beach.The number is 071 289370.

Each tour charges around $40.

Other tours operate from Rainbow Beach, the Sunshine Coast and Brisbane.

Sunstate Airlines fly guests to Orchid Beach airstrip from Brisbane, Maryborough and Hervey Bay. Charter aircraft can land here, as well as on Toby's Gap airstrip near Dilli Village. Neither is a public airstrip so permission is needed to land. Toby's Gap is run by the Department of Forestry.

ACCOMMODATION

Accommodation is available in the towns of Happy Valley and Eurong, Orchid Beach resort and Dilli Village.

Happy Valley is the largest settlement on the island, with flats and units for between $200 and $300 a week. It has a store which sells liquor, a public phone and a post box.

Eurong has a store, telephone and postal facility too. Its units, flats and cottages are let for around $385 a week per person with full board. Eurong also has a restaurant and a bar, although the latter has the atmosphere of a McDonalds.

Orchid Beach resort is a bit more upmarket, with units with full board for around $800. Their facilities include a restaurant, bar, shop and public telephone.

Dilli Village is leased privately through the Department of Forestry. It has no shop. Ring them on 071 279130 for more details.

If you've got the money, stay at Orchid Beach. If you don't, try Happy Valley.

CAMPING

On Fraser there are three types of camping to choose from.

Campgrounds with facilities are available at **Dundabara, Waddy Point** and **Wathumba** in the national park and at **Central Station, Lake Boomanjin, Lake McKenzie** and **Lake Allom** in the state forest. The cost is $7.50 a night or $45 maximum a week for a site.

Bush camping is okay between **Wathumba** and **Rooney Point** on the west coast of the national park and between **Orchid Beach** and **Ocean Lake** on the eastern side. Camping is allowed on any of the beaches around the state forest but not within 100 m of the lakes. The west coast can be particularly bad for sandflies, mosquitoes and march flies.

It is necessary to book for groups of over 15 people and for camps in the park.

There is a private camping ground at **Cathedral Beach**. No permits are required for this. Cathedral Beach has a shop with some takeaway food and public telephone. Their phone number is 071 279177.

The Fraser Island Recreation Board brochure *Fraser Island Guide* is recommended for a list of facilities at each of the campgrounds.

WALKING TRACKS

The most substantial walking track is the one beginning at Dilli and ending at Lake Wabby. Lake Boomanjin is the first lake encountered, about 7 km from Dilli. Lake Birrabeen is a further 10 km and Central Station another 6 km. From here it's a fairly steep climb to Basin Lake and undulating forest country to Lake McKenzie. This section of the walk is about 6 km long.

A track runs for 13 km to Lake Wabby through scrub. Here a huge sand blow is beginning to devour the lake. The ocean beach is reached by a 3 km track to the south-east.

Expect each kilometre to take between 15 and 20 minutes.

A shorter inland walk of around 5 km is between Orchid Beach and Ocean Lake. This walk is within the eastern beach camping zone of the national park.

A Sunmap of Fraser Island is recommended for walking.

CLOSEST DCPW OFFICE
Fraser Island Recreation Board and DCPW Office
Rainbow Beach Road
PO Box 30
Rainbow Beach 4
Queensland 4581
071 863160

There are DCPW Ranger Stations at Dundabara and Waddy Point on the island, as well as Department of Forestry Ranger Stations at Central Station, Eurong and Ungowa. Ces Neilsen at Central Station is particularly helpful.

NEAREST HELP
There are no medical services available on Fraser Island, but telephone boxes have instructions for emergency procedures on their inside walls or ring Hervey Bay Ambulance (071 281211) or Hervey Bay Police (071 283333). There are public telephones at Orchid Beach, Eurong, Happy Valley, Cathedral Beach and Dundabara and telephones available for emergencies at Ungowa, Central Station and Waddy Point.

Boats can call the Coast Guard on VH 4A ME and Air-Sea Rescue on VN 4 HV on the frequency of 27 MHZ.

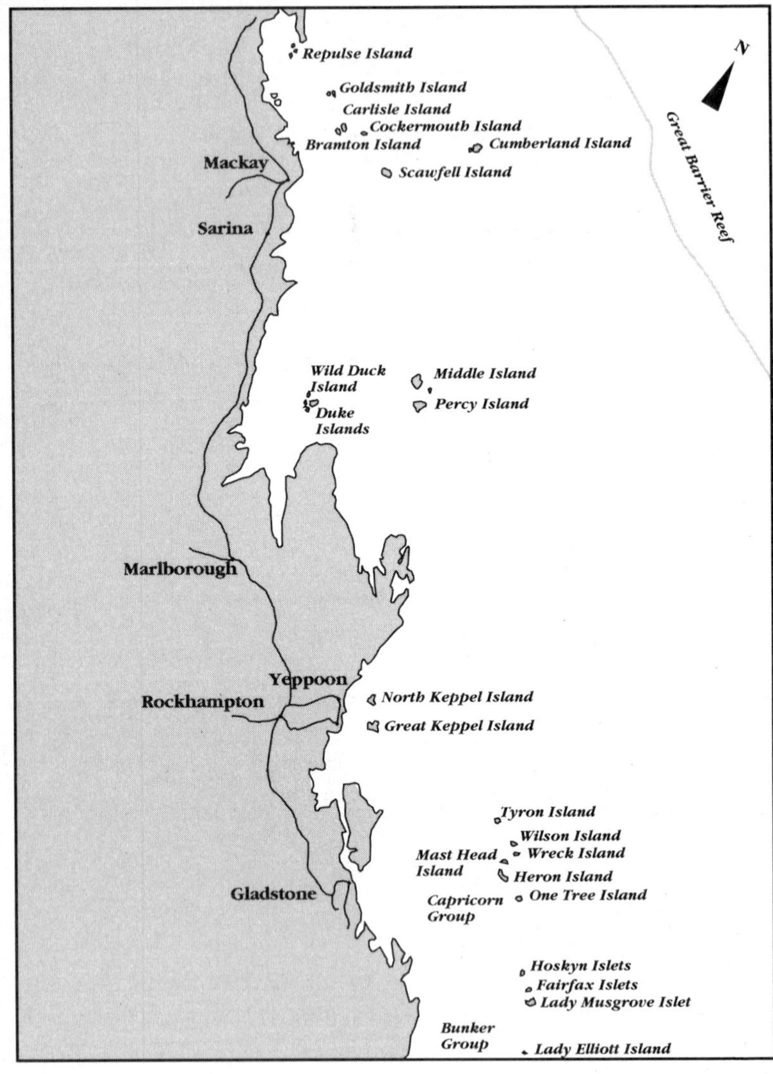

N
Repulse Island
Goldsmith Island
Carlisle Island
Cockermouth Island
Bramton Island
Cumberland Island
Mackay
Scawfell Island
Great Barrier Reef
Sarina
Wild Duck Island
Middle Island
Percy Island
Duke Islands
Marlborough
Yeppoon
Rockhampton
North Keppel Island
Great Keppel Island
Tyron Island
Wilson Island
Mast Head Island
Wreck Island
Heron Island
Gladstone
Capricorn Group
One Tree Island
Hoskyn Islets
Fairfax Islets
Lady Musgrove Islet
Bunker Group
Lady Elliott Island

The Southern Reef Islands

Many of the islands in this region are coral cays. Lady Elliot is the most southern coral cay — it sits on the southern extremity of the Great Barrier Reef.

Coral cays are formed on coral reefs when, through the action of the elements, coral rubble and sand accumulate to make a sandbar. Sea birds use the sandbar for nesting and fertilize the ground with guano. Vegetation follows, and a fully fledged coral cay is born.

Other islands in the region, such as Great Keppel and Newry, are continental islands. These islands were formed when the sea-level rose at the end of the last Ice Age drowning mainland mountain ranges. Most of these continental islands have their own fringing coral reefs.

The main centres of the region are Gladstone, Rockhampton and Mackay.

Lady Elliot Island

- **Resort**
- **Water**
- **Toilets**

Lady Elliot Island is a small coral cay on the southern tip of the Great Barrier Reef.

It is a casual family and dive resort with that away-from-it-all feel. Along with Heron and Lizard Islands, Lady Elliot specializes in diving and snorkelling. They charge $350 for a five-day diving certificate course on the island.

Because the island is within the Great Barrier Reef Marine Park, there is a limit placed on the number of guests in the resort. There is no organized night entertainment and no TV, so if really getting away from it all is what you want, this could be the island for you.

The Australian bêche-de-mer, or sea slug, industry began on the island last century. It was then used by the Japanese as a source of guano, or bird droppings, for fertilizer. Lady Elliot's lighthouse dates back to 1866.

ACCESS

Sunstate Airlines do the 80 km trip from Bundaberg daily. The flight takes 35 minutes and the island has its own airstrip.

Contact:

Sunstate Travel Centre
Bourbong street
Bundaberg
Queensland 4670
071 716077

See them about day tours of the island for $170.

ACCOMMODATION

The small resort has room for 120 guests in three types of accommodation. Two adults sharing a Safari Tent or Bunkhouse will pay $725 per person for a week and the Reef Units with private facilities will cost $970. This includes return air transfers from Bundaberg and meals.

The resort's address is:
Mail Bag No.6
Bundaberg
Queensland 4670

Bookings: 008 072200 or 071 716077

The administration number on the mainland is 071 551266.

NEAREST HELP

The nearest emergency help is at Bundaberg and the island is in 24-hour radio contact with them.

Bunker Islands

The Bunker Islands are a series of coral cays between Lady Elliot and Heron Islands. The national park island of **Lady Musgrave** is the only one open to campers. The small, flat island is an important breeding ground for the loggerhead and green turtles and the mutton-bird and white-capped noddy.

The vegetation of pisonia trees ringed by casuarina and pandanus was virtually wiped out by introduced goats until they were removed in 1971. It is still recovering.

The deep entrance to the atoll-type lagoon was said to be dug by Japanese fishermen at the turn of the century.

- **National Park (category C)**
- **Campground**
- **Bush camping**
- **Toilets**

Lady Musgrave Island

Lady Musgrave Island has a campground with pit toilets but it is necessary to carry in water, and wood or fuel for cooking. The island has harmless centipedes but bird ticks should be removed if you're unlucky enough to get one. Lady Musgrave permits cost $2 per person per night.

Fairfax Island

Fairfax Island is for day visits only. Suffering from the scars of mining, goats and Air Force practice bombing, it is slowly recovering.

Hoskyn Island

Hoskyn Island is the most unspoiled and least visited in the group but is for day visits only.

ACCESS

The *Lady Musgrave* leaves Burnett Heads near Bundaberg at 8.45 a.m. each Tuesday, Thursday, Saturday and Sunday for Lady Musgrave Island. The cost is $75 return. Ring 071 529011 for details.

Other boats are available for charter in Gladstone. Gladstone Promotion and Development Limited has a list of charter operators. Their address: 56 Goondoon Street, Gladstone Queensland 4680, 079 724000.

CLOSEST DCPW OFFICE

Gladstone District Office
Roseberry Street
PO Box 315
Gladstone
Queensland 4680
079 761621
Rockhampton office 079 276511.

NEAREST HELP

Heron Island clinic or Gladstone

Heron Island

- **National Park**
- **Resort**
- **Water**
- **Toilets**
- **Phone**
- **Ranger staff**
- **Walking tracks**
- **Suitable for disabled**

Heron Island resort specializes in diving. It has its own diving course which lasts seven days and costs $220. However, it doesn't encourage solo diving and insists everyone take the resort boat.

The island is a true coral cay, 17 hectares, with its own research station and DCPW information centre (079 725690).

It is a place for the nature lover, with many birds, such as reef herons, white-capped noddies and wedge-tailed shearwaters or mutton-birds, all squawking in the pisonia forest that covers the island. Heron Island is also the breeding ground of the green turtle between October and February.

Not known for its nightlife, the island nevertheless has a disco and movies. An added blessing is that there are no swarms of day-trippers to overcrowd the tiny island.

ACCESS

Heron Island is 72 km out to sea. There is a daily catamaran called *Reef Adventurer II* that leaves from the Gladstone Marina at 8 a.m. and 1.30 p.m. It costs $130 return or $65 return standby.

If you think the boat trip is a touch too long, there's a half-hour helicopter ride from Gladstone for $290 return.

ACCOMMODATION

Heron Island can accommodate 250 guests in four ways. The Lodges — bunk style accommodation for the budget conscious — cost $700 for an adult sharing for a week. Reef Suites cost $1085, Heron Suites $1170 and the exotic Beachhouses $1240.

Standby rates are $80 a night for the Lodges and $65 return for the launch.

You can book by ringing the P & O office in Brisbane on 07 2688224 or contact Gladstone Travel World

124 Goondoon Street
Gladstone
Queensland 4680.
079 722288.

NEAREST HELP

Gladstone, by helicopter, or the island clinic.

Capricorn Islands

- **National Park (category C)**
- **Resort**
- **Campground**
- **Bush camping**
- **Toilets**

The Capricorn Islands include North West, Tryon and Masthead Islands. There are campgrounds on each. Heron Island is a member of the group but has been covered separately.

North West Island

North West Island is the biggest coral cay on the Great Barrier Reef — 91 hectares. Formerly used as a site to collect guano and then for a turtle cannery, the island is infested with cats and chickens.

It has a designated camping area and pit toilets. The hut on the beach has some water but campers are advised to take their own in. A track runs across the island from the hut. The camping area is often fully booked at holiday periods, but there is a privately run backpackers' camping area on the island as well. Ring 079 336350 for details.

Tryon Island

Tryon Island is another typical cay with much birdlife. The black-naped and bridled terns are prominent here. Only 11 hectares in area, it has had little disturbance from humans. There are no toilets, and generators are not permitted on Tryon or Masthead Island. Tryon, Masthead and North West Islands are national parks. Permits cost $2 per head per night.

Wilson and Erskine Islands

Wilson and Erskine Islands are day-visit islands only.

Wreck Island is a Preservation Zone and **One Tree Island** has been set aside for research. There is no access to either.

ACCESS

The Aristocat operates from Gladstone to Masthead and North West Islands for day trips and does drop-offs for any of the local islands. They do dives as well. Ring Robin Cannon on 079 725326. The boat is fast.

Reef Seeker leaves from Yeppoon for North West Island for day trips and drop-offs. It costs $70 return. Ring 079 336744.

For a list of charter boat operators,.contact:
Gladstone Promotion and Development Limited
56 Goondoon Street
Gladstone Queensland 4680
079 724000.

CAMPING

Camping is permitted on North West, Tryon and Masthead Islands. All campers are asked to take in their own water and take out their rubbish. The feeding of seagulls disturbs the ecological balance and camping should be avoided on the foredunes. Turtles nest on the islands between October and February and care should be taken not to disturb them. Masthead Island has bush camping only.

CLOSEST DCPW OFFICE
Gladstone District Office
Roseberry Street
PO Box 315
Gladstone
Queensland 4680
079 761621

The staff of this office are often in the field, so try the Rockhampton office on 079 276511 if no-one is there.

NEAREST HELP
Heron Island clinic or Gladstone.

Quoin Island

Quoin Island, only 5 km from the industrial city of Gladstone, is primarily a quiet spot for the locals to get away to. But it's different, and it's away from the crowds.

It doesn't have very good beaches. The east side is rocky with grey sand interludes, and the west coast is mostly mangroves. But the island's 35 hectares offers some good walks along its eastern shoreline and down to the southern point.

The owner of the resort bought the whole island and sub-divided the middle portion for holiday houses. The original owner, Lewis Allen, retained a small block on the northern tip. He was stationed in Gladstone during World War II and moved there after the war. He built the rock walls that form part of the lounge and were once part of the original resort.

- **Resort**
- **Water**
- **Toilets**
- **Phone**
- **Walking tracks**

Curtis Island and Facing Island

Curtis Island

Curtis Island is a big island north of Quoin that has a small holiday settlement on its south-east corner. Southend, as it's called, has a permanent population of 12. It has a licensed general store and basic accommodation at the Capricorn Lodge (079 724811). Southend offers a picnic area and free camping.

Facing Island

Facing Island, to the east of Quoin, has a picnic and camping area 2 km north of Farmers Point wharf called the Oaks. There

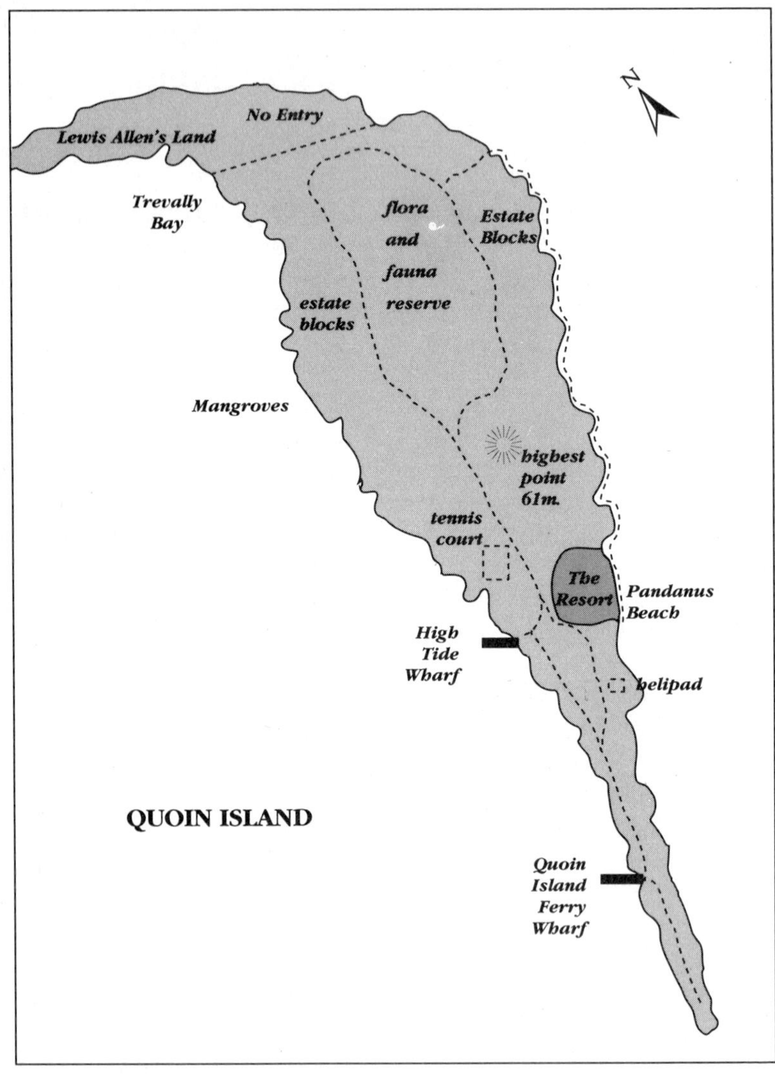
N
No Entry
Lewis Allen's Land
Trevally Bay
flora and fauna reserve
Estate Blocks
estate blocks
Mangroves
highest point 61m.
tennis court
The Resort
Pandanus Beach
High Tide Wharf
helipad
QUOIN ISLAND
Quoin Island Ferry Wharf

are no facilities apart from some tables.

The ferry *Calypso* goes to Southend and Farmers Point on Fridays, Saturdays and Sundays for $8 return. Ring 079 721261 for details.

ACCESS

The Quoin Island ferry leaves O'Connell wharf in Gladstone daily at 9.30 a.m. and returns at 3.30 p.m Day trips cost $20 and include lunch.

Bookings and enquiries on 079 722283.

ACCOMMODATION

The resort at Quoin has a pleasant lodge-type atmosphere with big lounges, carpets and rock walls. Beyond the lounge there's a bar and restaurant, and near the beach, a good-sized pool.

There are eight self-contained suites, well-priced at $69 a night. And that's with three meals a day. But don't expect Hayman Island at that cost!

Bookings: PO Box 129
Gladstone Queensland 4680
079 722283

NEAREST HELP

Gladstone.
There is a helipad on Quoin Island.

Great Keppel Island

North Keppel, Pumpkin, Humpy, Miall, Middle, Halfway, Pelican, Divide, and Peak Islands

- National Park (category B and C)
- Resort
- Campground
- Water
- Toilets
- Picnic area
- Fireplace
- Phone
- Walking tracks
- Suitable for disabled
- YHA

Great Keppel Island has two big positive points. It has the best beaches of any Queensland resort island and the best choice of cheap accommodation.

Australian Airlines, which runs the resort, has been promoting it as a place for young people for years, though it seems they are now trying to attract the family back.But the island will remain the young people's island because of its beaches and it's so cheap.

The island offers five kinds of accommodation that are less expensive than the resort (see under Accommodation and Camping).

At about 1500 hectares, Great or South Keppel Island is the largest island in the Keppel group. Settled in 1906, the island has an inglorious history. The original graziers were responsible for poisoning the flour of the island Aborigines with strychnine after some of the graziers' sheep were killed.

The resort was opened in the 1960s. The island has 17 beaches and offers good diving and snorkelling. There is a dive shop at **Wapparaburra Haven** and snorkel gear is available from the resort for $8 a day. **Monkey Beach** has good coral.

The resort has parasailing — 5 minutes in the air will cost you $20.

Svendsen's Beach is a popular anchorage with yachties and notices often appear on the Haven noticeboard for crew.

N
Big Peninsula
Butterfish
Bay
Little
Peninsula
Svendsen
Svendsen's Beach
Middle
Island
Wreck Beach
Leeke's Beach
Bald
Rock
Putney Beach
Wapparaburra
Haven
Camping Area
Lookout
Leeke's
Homestead
Dam
Bald Rock Pt
Light-
house
Fishermans
Beach
Resort
Mt Wyndham
Air
Strip
Red Beach
Calm Beach
Shelving Beach
Monkey Beach
Long
Beach
Monkey Point
Little Monkey Point
Halfway Island
Humpy Island
GREAT KEPPEL ISLAND

The resort allows campers and hostellers to use its cafe, souvenir shop and the infamous Wreck Bar. The bar offers a band, disco and video clips (where else on the Queensland coast could you see Hunters and Collectors on video?) but the cafe has cappuccino that looks and tastes like dishwater.

If you enjoy drinking, bring your own because it's expensive to take away at the bar.

North Keppel Island

North Keppel Island is a national park which has a camping area at **Considine Beach** on the north-western side. There is a creek and a well but none of the water is suitable for drinking. It also has a septic toilet.

South of Considine Beach is a collection of cabins. You can have one of them for $230 a week by contacting Brian Hooper Real Estate in Yeppoon on 079 393841. The cabins have refrigerators, gas burners and tank water.

Take insect repellent to North Keppel.

Pumpkin Island

Close to North Keppel is a small privately owned island called **Pumpkin Island**. It has some small, six-bunk cabins for $10 a night or $60 a week. Frequented mainly by local families for fishing, it is popular with southerners as well. It is quiet and has no power but has gas. A water taxi costs around $36 return. Ring 079 392431 for bookings and 079 336350 for the water taxi.

Humpy Island

Humpy Island is a small national park island close to Great Keppel. It has 30 campsites with a toilet and water tank. North Keppel and Humpy Island have a category B classification.

Miall, Middle, Halfway, Pelican, Divided and Peak Islands

Other national park islands in the Keppel group suitable for camping are **Miall**, **Middle and Halfway Islands**, each of which has one good beach and, further south, **Pelican**, **Divided** and **Peak Islands**. All these islands have a category C fee.

Camping is not permitted on Peak Island during turtle season. Pelican and Divided Islands are very rocky. There are limited anchorages and few beaches on these three islands. None of the islands have facilities.

Wedge and Hummocky Islands are privately owned.

ACCESS

Most people get the *Victory* catamaran from Rosslyn Bay, a few kilometres south of Yeppoon. It leaves at 9.10a.m. and costs $23 return. Included in the cost is a cruise around part of Great Keppel. In good weather it visits the underwater observatory off Middle Island. It costs $8.

There is a daily parking charge at Rosslyn Bay or try the Kempsea Car Park, near the harbour, on 079 336670. Buses connect Yeppoon with boat services from Rosslyn Bay.

Great Keppel Island Tourist Services also operate the faster aquajet which leaves at 9.30 a.m., 11 a.m. and 3.30 p.m. It costs $20 return. Ring them on 079 336744 for information about their services.

Water taxis provide a regular service to the islands. Try the *Ariake* (079 336350).

Sunstate Airlines operate a service to Great Keppel from Rockhampton.

A six-berth bareboat is available for charter from Yeppoon for around $140 a day. Ring 079 336577.

ACCOMMODATION

There are three types of indoor accommodation on the island. There is a Youth Hostel near Wapparaburra Haven that houses about 55 people. It's often crowded so booking is needed. Everyone is asked to book in person at the Rockhampton Hostel, but I didn't find this was necessary. Their number is 079 394341. For $9 a night you'll get rooms with up to 12 bunks in them and concrete floors — definitely not in the five-star category. Its banksia and gum forest location is the best thing about it. There's a five night-limit.

A little more up-market is the resort. There you'll pay $882 a week for the Garden Units and $1050 for the Beach Front ones. It's a big resort with room for 400 guests. Their number is 079 391744. The resort has day-visiting facilities at 'The Anchorage'.

There are also cabins at the Wapparaburra Haven for $50 per night.

The closest cheap mainland places are the Yeppoon Backpackers, a converted motel with its own pool, sundeck and restaurant (079 392122), and the Rockhampton Youth Hostel. This has a sterile, army-camp atmosphere but it's clean and has good facilities. Situated just over the river from the town centre, it's handy to the Capricorn Coach Terminal. The managers are nice — they just need an interior decorator! Telephone 079 275288.

CAMPING

On the spit that separates Fishermans Beach from Putney Beach is **Wapparaburra Haven**. It takes its name from the Aboriginal word for the island meaning 'resting place'.

Middle Island from the road to Leeke's Beach, Great Keppel Island.

The Haven is quite independent of the resort because the land it occupies is run by the local shire. It has its own bistro and kiosk, which sells everything from ice-creams to lentilburgers.

There are 35 campsites at the Haven for $7 per person per night and 40 established tents for $12 a night. Their telephone number is 079 391907.

The Camping Connection offers packages for campers aged 18 to 35. It has its own 'precinct' adjacent to the Youth Hostel and the Haven and it supplies all meals and activities. They charge $360 for a week in low season. Ring 008 030711 for details.

WALKING TRACKS

Great Keppel Island is blessed with a good choice of walking tracks.

If lonely beaches are what you're after, try **Leekes Beach**. The 2 km walk will take around 40 minutes. Some maps have a track marked along Putney Creek. It is barely discernible and the creek is full of rubbish, so take the bitumen road out of the resort and walk up a fairly steep hill to a lookout. There's another steep track down to the beach, only rougher. An alternative way back is along the mudflats behind the beach.

The old homestead is another kilometre down the track and the lighthouse is 6 km away.

The tracks leading to **Shelving, Monkey**

and **Long** beaches start at the southern end of Fishermans Beach, just past the resort.

CLOSEST DCPW OFFICE

Regional Office
194 Quay Street
PO Box 1395
Rockhampton
Queensland 4700
079 276511

or the DCPW office at
Rosslyn Bay Harbour
PO Box 770
Yeppoon
Queensland 4703
079 336608

NEAREST HELP

There are nurses at the resort and an air ambulance to Rockhampton.

Duke Islands

The **Duke Islands** suffer from several disadvantages. One is the absence of jumping-off points along the coast. The most obvious access point for private boats is **Stanage Bay**, but there is a long dirt road to the settlement. Another disadvantage is the extent of the tides — up to 7 metres.

• **Bush camping**

Yet another put-off is the closeness to the Shoalwater Bay Military Training area.

Wild Duck Island

Wild Duck Island, which has an airstrip, has been trying to be a resort for years but was, at the time of writing, in receivership. It is known locally as Lame Duck Island.

Many of the islands are privately owned. Most yachties miss the group of islands altogether and head for the Percy Isles instead.

Percy Isles

There is no easy access to the **Percy Isles** either, except by private boat.

Middle Percy is a popular stopover for yachties. It's roughly halfway between the Keppels and the Whitsundays. The island is used as a sheep run.

Surrounded by sandy bays, the island is known as a good anchorage with washing and shower facilities for visitors.

Andy Martin lives on the island and allows people to stay in his A-frame building on the west side. He can be contacted by writing:

C/- Mackay Post Office
Queensland 4740

- **Bush camping**
- **Water**

Cumberland Islands

- **National Park (category C)**
- **Campground**
- **Bush camping**
- **Toilets**
- **Picnic area**
- **Fireplace**

All of the Cumberland Islands are national parks except for Keswick, St Bees and part of Farrier.

Brampton Island has a resort, and is covered in the next section along with its close neighbour **Carlisle**.

St Bees is a private island that was once run by the Busuttin family as a sheep property. The family began Brampton resort in 1933.

Scawfell Island

There are four islands suitable for camping in the Cumberland group, and **Scawfell Island** is one of them. Lying about 115 km north-west of Middle Percy and 50 km north-east of Mackay, the island has a safe anchorage on its northern side. Called **Refuge Bay**, there is a beach and campsite here with no facilities and water only in summer. At 1090 hectares, Scawfell is the largest island of the group. It's a popular yachtie stopover.

Cockermouth Island

Cockermouth Island has a good anchorage and sandy beach on its west side. The island is 40 km from Mackay. There are campsites on the north-western beach with no facilities or water.

Goldsmith Island

North-west of Cockermouth, in the Sir James Smith Group, is **Goldsmith Island.** Again, there is a good anchorage and campsites on the north-western side of the island. It has excellent beaches, facilities but no water. To the west of Goldsmith lies **South Repulse Island**. There is a campground on the western beach with some facilities but no water.

Repulse Island

ACCESS

Roylens may do drop-offs to certain islands on their way from Mackay to the Whitsundays. Ring them on 079 553066.

The boat *Tsarina* is available for charter from Mackay. It also offers three-day trips to the reef for around $270. Their number is 079 551797.

A seaplane can be chartered from Fredrickson's Aerial Services in Mackay (079 423161).

If you just want to see the islands from above, North Queensland Aerial Services can help (079 511510).

See Tourism Mackay Inc. (079 522677) or the Queensland Travel Centre (079 572292) for more information on boat and plane charters.

CAMPING

Scawfell Island has some sites, no facilities and you'll need to take water in summer.

Cockermouth Island has some sites, no facilities and no water.

Goldsmith Island has some campsites as well as toilets, tables and barbecues but no water.

South Repulse Island has some sites and similar facilitiesto Goldsmith, but no water.

CLOSEST DCPW OFFICE

Mackay District Office
64 Victoria Street
PO Box 623
Mackay
Queensland 4740.
079 576292.

NEAREST HELP

To Scawfell Island: St Bees Island (20 km).

To Cockermouth Island: Brampton Island (13 km).

To Goldsmith Island: Brampton Island (20 km), or Farrier Island (nearby private island).

To South Repulse Island: Midge Point (15 km).

Brampton Island

Carlisle Island

- **National Park (category C)**
- **Resort**
- **Water**
- **Toilets**
- **Picnic area**
- **Fireplace**
- **Phone**
- **Walking tracks**
- **Suitable for disabled**

B**rampton Island**, along with the other islands of the Cumberland group, derives its name from a Lakes District town in England.

Brampton Island is a national park with a resort, owned and run by Australian Airlines. It has fringing coral around its 770 hectares, but is not part of the Great Barrier Reef as it is a continental island. It has some magnificent walks,the best is 'the circuit walk'.

The massive figtree outside the old recreation hall dates back to 1933, the year the resort was opened by the Busuttin family. The guests in those days were offered sports that mostly involved the killing of the local wildlife, such as turtle hunting, crocodile shooting and manta-ray harpooning.

The island was declared a national park in 1936.

Day-visitors are welcome. There are two picnic areas at **Turtle Bay** and near **Clump Point**. Turtle Bay is the easiest to get to.with showers and water provided at the resort.

See under Camping for information about camping on nearby **Carlisle Island**.

ACCESS

The *Spirit of Roylen* makes the 40-minute run to Brampton from Mackay harbour every day at 9 a.m., except for Tuesday, when it leaves at 10 a.m. The cost is $24 return. The crossing can be rough in heavy seas.

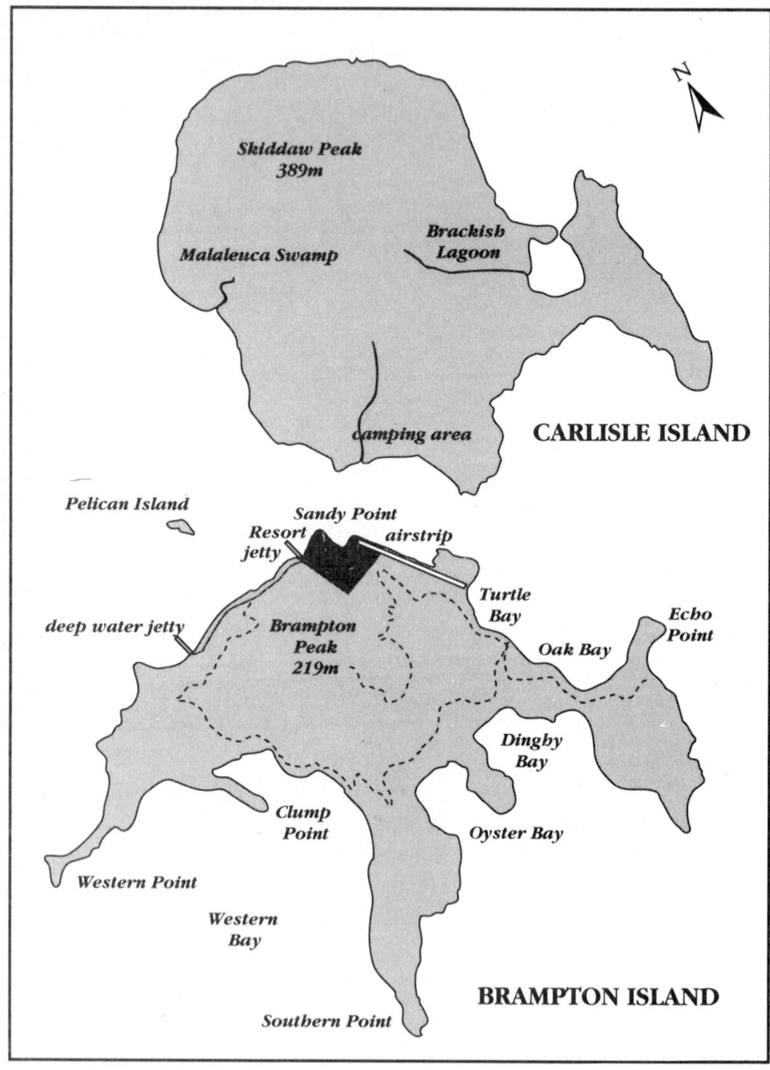
N
Skiddaw Peak
389m
Brackish
Lagoon
Malaleuca Swamp
camping area
CARLISLE ISLAND
Pelican Island
Sandy Point
Resort
jetty
airstrip
Turtle
Bay
Echo
Point
deep water jetty
Brampton
Peak
219m
Oak Bay
Dingby
Bay
Clump
Point
Oyster Bay
Western Point
Western
Bay
BRAMPTON ISLAND
Southern Point

The same boat goes to Hamilton and Lindeman Islands on certain days. Ring Roylen Cruises (079 553066).

Australian Regional Airlines can fly you to Brampton from Mackay in 15 minutes.

ACCOMMODATION

Brampton resort is fairly large with 100 rooms and 240 beds. It has an informal, family atmosphere. The new entertainment and dining building and Blue Lagoon units are transforming from one of Queensland's oldest island resorts.

For an adult sharing in low season the Blue Lagoon units will cost $1134 a week.There is a standby rate of $98 per person per night.
The resort's number is 079 514499.

CAMPING

Camping is not permitted on Brampton, but there are 15 sites at **Southern Bay** on **Carlisle Island**. It's possible to walk across to Carlisle at low tide, otherwise the resort will ferry people, but it is necessary to ring them before leaving the mainland.

Carlisle Island

There are no facilities and water has to be carried in. Permits from Mackay DCPW.

WALKING TRACKS

Brampton Island's **circuit walk** is a must. The walk takes you through a tropical wonderland of Moreton Bay ash and poplar gum forests, giant grasstrees, coral beaches and sweeping panoramas. It is an intermediate type walk with a steep climb from the last beach back to the resort.

The start of the walking track is near the resort's golf course. Once you reach Turtle Bay, follow the signs to Dinghy Bay. Soon after crossing a four-wheel drive track is a sign reading 'Island Circuit — 5 km', followed by another sign reading 'Dinghy Bay — 0.7 km'.

The walk to Dinghy Bay, then Echo Point and return, takes around two and a half hours. The circuit walk is around 7 km and takes about 3-hours. For mountainclimbers, there's the steep track to Brampton Peak, taking 2 hours for a 4 km round trip.

REGULAR SERVICES TO OTHER ISLANDS

The *Spirit of Roylen* runs to Hamilton and Lindeman Islands 3 days a week and may do drop-offs to islands along the way.

CLOSEST DCPW OFFICE

Mackay District Office
64 Victoria Street
PO Box 623
Mackay
Queensland 4740.
079 576292.

NEAREST HELP

Resort nurse or Mackay.

Newry Island

Rabbit Island and Outer Newry Island

- **National Park (category B)**
- **Resort**
- **Campground**
- **Water**
- **Toilets**
- **Picnic area**
- **Fireplace**
- **Phone**
- **Walking tracks**

Newry Island is unique. David Haig, Mackay lawyer and yachtsman, describes it as Queensland's 'last earthy resort'.

There are three groups of people who frequent Newry. Most of the guests are coalminers, cane cockies (sugar farmers) or fishermen. Then come the Mackay locals and, lastly, the tourists. Backpackers take note!

It has one of the best anchorages and protected harbours on the coast, so it is popular with yachties too. There was talk of making it Mackay's harbour before the city fathers built the artificial one.

Put simply, it is the nicest and most unpretentious island resort you'll see in Queensland. It is small, accommodating only 30 people, and inexpensive. There is a licensed bar but no entertainment — but who needs it?

There is a superb walk through patches of rainforest to a picnic area on the other side of the island. You may see a few koalas along the way. They have been known to swim between Newry Island and nearby Rabbit and Outer Newry Islands.

However, the island does have a few negative points. Its beaches are not very good and new arrivals are forced to get their feet wet as there is no jetty. These things just add to the flavour of this unique island!

The resort has some campsites, but

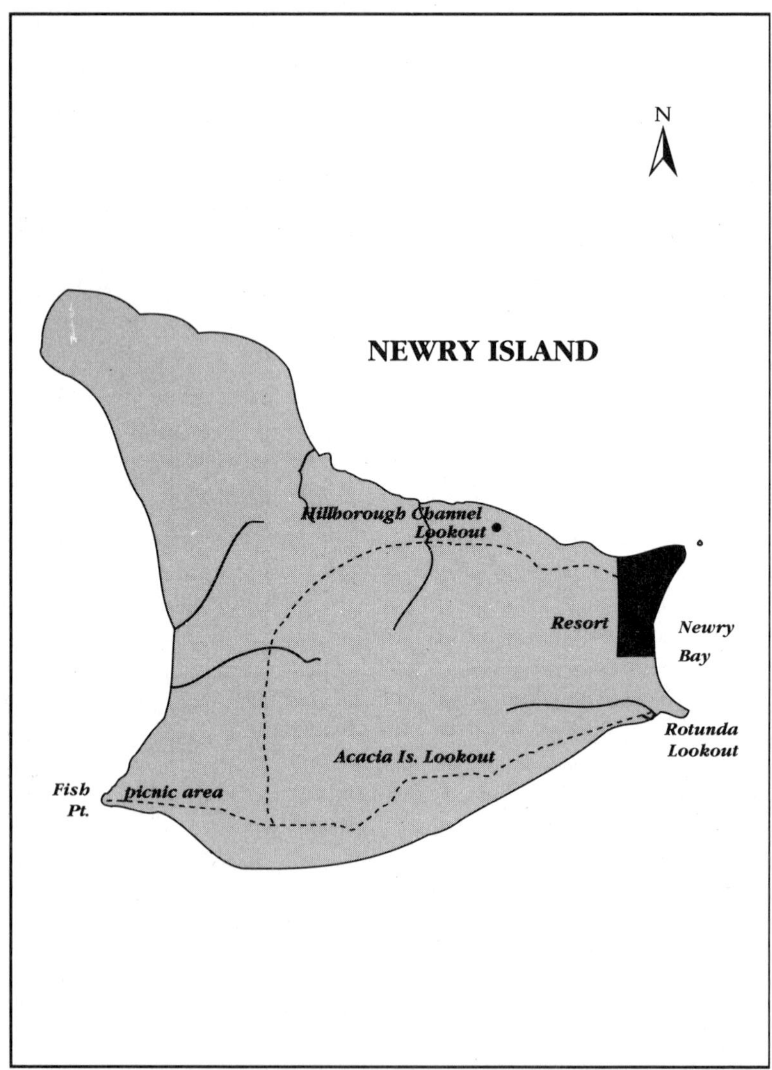
N
NEWRY ISLAND
Hillborough Channel
Lookout
Resort
Newry
Bay
Rotunda
Lookout
Acacia Is. Lookout
Fish
Pt.
picnic area

otherwise there is no camping on the island.

The resort will take campers to **Rabbit Island**, which has good beaches and a camping area on its south-east corner or **Outer Newry** where there is a camping area on its western beach. Both campgrounds have facilities such as toilets and tables, and water. Permits require a category B fee.

Rabbit Island

Outer Newry Island

ACCESS

The resort picks up people on the coast at Victor Creek, near Seaforth, a coastal holiday town north of Mackay. The cost is $10 return. Ring the resort on 079 590214.

ACCOMMODATION

The resort offers spartan bunk-style accommodation in a stone cabin for $15 a night per person.

There are self contained units as well. These cost $30 per person per night or $60 full board.

The resort's address is:
PO Box 3 Seaforth
Queensland 4741
079 590214

CAMPING

The resort has 20 camping sites for $7 per person per night.

The resort staff will take you out to Rabbit or Outer Newry Islands too (see main text).

WALKING TRACKS

The walking track around the island, and down to Fish Point, is highly recommended. About a 3 km round trip, the grade is intermediate overall and has a lovely picnic area halfway at Fish Point, overlooking the Rabbit Island camping area. Water, toilets and tables are provided. Start at the Rotunda lookout.

CLOSEST DCPW OFFICE

Mackay District Office
64 Victoria Street
PO Box 623
Mackay
Queensland 4740
079 576292

NEAREST HELP

Seaforth (5 km), or Mackay Air-sea Rescue.

Newry Beach.

The Whitsundays

The Whitsunday group gets more visitors than any other islands and is the fastest-growing area on the Queensland coast. Airlie Beach is the over-busy mainland centre of activity. Shute Harbour or Shutehaven is the main port. Proserpine and Hamilton Island are the two main domestic airports.

It's understandable that the Whitsundays are so popular. The natural beauty of the area, with the rugged Conway National Park on the mainland and the thickly forested mountains of the islands, is one reason. The predictable winds and protected waters make the area a safe one to sail in, and earn it a reputation as the yacht-charter capital of Australia. Many of the islands have their own coral reefs. The group is well situated for visits to the Great Barrier Reef, the climate is good and there is a wide choice of island resorts and camping areas. There are 91 national park islands between Mackay and Bowen; 25 of them have camping areas.

The Whitsundays havesome of the clearest

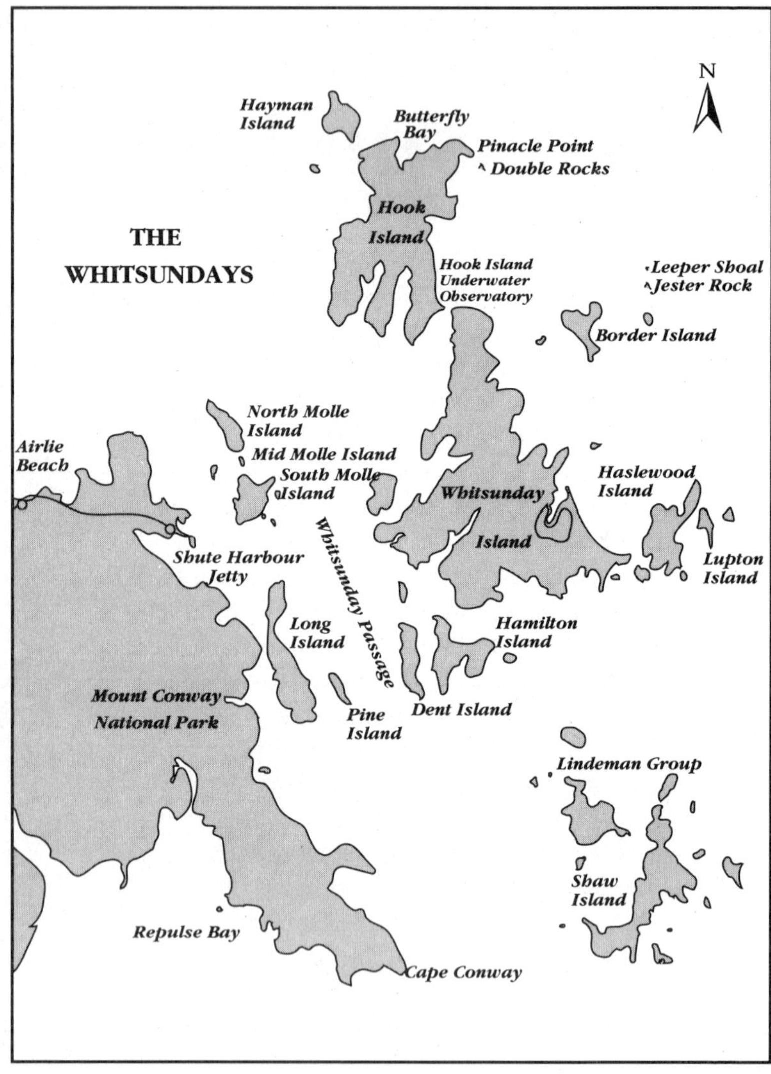
N
Hayman
Island
Butterfly
Bay
Pinacle Point
Double Rocks
Hook
Island
THE
WHITSUNDAYS
Hook Island
Underwater
Observatory
Leeper Shoal
Jester Rock
Border Island
North Molle
Island
Airlie
Beach
Mid Molle Island
South Molle
Island
Whitsunday
Island
Haslewood
Island
Whitsunday Passage
Shute Harbour
Jetty
Lupton
Island
Long
Island
Hamilton
Island
Mount Conway
National Park
Pine
Island
Dent Island
Lindeman Group
Shaw
Island
Repulse Bay
Cape Conway

water in Australia. Because there is no farming close to the coast, there is no soil or organic material being carried down rivers to the sea. so it's ideal for diving and snorkelling. However, tidal variation can be up to 6 metres, so the area isn't renowned for its beaches.

The islands were formed over 10 000 years ago at the end of the Ice Age. Ice melted, the sea-level rose and coastal mountain ranges were isolated to form the continental islands of the Whitsundays.

There is a choice of ways to see them. The big cruise boats, such as South Molle's *Capricorn*, leave Shute Harbour every day, for trips to the resort islands. Or there are the smaller yachts such as *Gretel* or *Banjora* that tour certain islands or reefs. If neither of these choices appeals to you, you can charter your own boat or yacht.

Getting around the islands is big business. There are as many day cruises, yacht-charter and boat hire operators as there are islands.

Two of the more up-market yachts are the America's Cup challenger *Gretel* and the maxi-yacht *Apollo*. *Gretel* ends up at Langford Reef, near Hayman Island, so it is one for the divers and snorkellers. *Apollo* takes you to Whitehaven Beach on Whitsunday Island so it is a good one for the swimmers and sunbakers. The *Banjora* is an old motor-sailer that does one-day dives at Manta Ray Bay off Hook Island. It drops off campers at Butterfly Bay as well. On weekends it does trips to the outer reef. Expect to pay between $20 and $40 for any of the day cruises.

There is a staggering choice of day trips and charter companies and too many to list here.

For information about any of the day-cruise boats, contact:

Mandy's Mine of Information
Roundabout Shops
Shute Harbour Road
Airlie Beach
Queensland 4802
079 466848 or 008 075138

And for details about yacht charter see the Whitsunday Tourism Association's publication *Travel Agents' Handbook* for a complete list of crewed charters, bareboats, boat hire and provisioners. Their address is:

PO Box 83
Airlie Beach
Queensland 4802
079 466673.

Note that bareboats come in all sizes from 6

to 14 metres, and that there are restrictions on how far bareboats of less than 10 metres can go.

Anyone contemplating cruising the Whitsundays should get a copy of *100 Magic Miles of the Great Barrier Reef* by David Colfelt for everything you wanted to know about the islands and more. See particularly the 'Boating in the Whitsundays' chapter.

Scuba diving is another growth industry. Tropic Isle Motel has a dive shop which offers the PADI scuba course for $285. Ring Oceania Dive on 079 466032 or check out the local Yellow Pages.

CLOSEST DCPW OFFICE

PO Box 332
Airlie Beach
Queensland 4802
079 469430

Alternatively, see them in person at the Ranger Station in Conway National Park, opposite the base camping area on Shute Harbour Road.

The national park islands have a category C fee.

See Mandy's Mine of Information about being dropped off at your chosen camping area by one of the day-cruise boats, or hitch a ride with a private yacht. If all else fails, ring Whitsunday Water Taxi (079 469202) or Seair Pacific for air-taxi service (079 469133). A bus service operates between Proserpine and Shute Harbour. Ring Samson Tours (079 452377) for timetable details.

NEAREST HELP

At clinics in Airlie Beach (079 466241 or 079 466275) or Proserpine Hospital (079 451422).

Air-sea Rescue and the Coast Guard are available on 27.88 MHZ with the call signs VJ 4 TF and VH 4 AFZ respectively.

Lindeman Island

Lindeman Island boasts seven beaches, 20 km of walking tracks and a 500 hectare national park.

Angus Nicholson bought the lease on Lindeman Island in 1923 with the idea of building some rooms for tourists. Opened in 1929, it was Queensland's first island resort.

Lindeman was sold in 1986 to a Sydney businessman. He has built 104 new suites and kept it as a predominantly family resort but widened the market to include budget accommodation.

The island offers a unique Adventure Island programme for children between 8 and 14 years which takes them away for camping trips and lessons in bushcraft. There is a golf course at the resort.

Thomas Island and Shaw Island

- **National Park (category C)**
- **Resort**
- **Campground**
- **Bush camping**
- **Water**
- **Toilets**
- **Picnic area**
- **Fireplace**
- **Phone**
- **Walking tracks**

Thomas Island

To the south-east of Lindeman is the beautiful but isolated **Thomas Island.** It has campsites with facilities, but no water, on **Sea Eagle Beach** on the south-eastern side of the island. There are good anchorages here, and at the campground at **Naked Lady Beach** to the north-west. The island is about 45 km from Shute Harbour and 15 km from Lindeman Island.

Shaw Island

Closer to Lindeman lies the large rocky **Shaw Island**. There are undeveloped campsites with no water or facilities at **Neck Bay** facing the eastern tip of Lindeman, and at **Burning Point**, which is at the south-western end of the island. Both have good anchorages but the beaches dry out at low tide.

ACCESS

There are water taxis to Hamilton Island, and light aircraft to Proserpine, to connect with Australian Airlines flights; to Hamilton Island to connect with Ansett; and to Mackay.

Ring the resort (079 469333) for all details.

ACCOMMODATION

For two adults sharing in low season, the Seaforth Suites will cost $2520 each a week, the Whitsunday Waterfronts $2030 and the Whitsunday Hillsides $1890.

Reservations can be made by ringing the resort (008 075155 or 079 469333).

CLOSEST DCPW OFFICE

For all the Whitsunday islands, contact:
Whitsunday Office
PO Box 332
Airlie Beach
Queensland 4802
079 469430

NEAREST HELP

Hamilton Island

Long Island

Long Island is a 1030-hectare island with three small resorts on its western side.

- **National Park**
- **Resort**
- **Campground**
- **Water**
- **Toilets**
- **Picnic area**
- **Fireplace**
- **Phone**
- **Walking tracks**

Contiki's Whitsunday Resort, once called Whitsunday 100 and before that Happy Bay, is a recently revamped resort aimed at the 18 to 35 age group. Only 8 km south-east of Shute Harbour, it's a popular anchorage with yachties and bareboaters. The resort has its own restaurant, disco, gym, sauna and spa and lots of organized fun.

A 15 minute walk south of here is **Palm Bay**. Low-key and low-budget, the resort owned by Australian Pacific Tours, spans a narrow neck of the island with a coral beach on the western shore and a pebble beach on the other. It has its own general store, with a limited range of products, and sells evening meals — usually barbecued flesh and salad. There are moorings available. A nice spot.

Soon to be rebuilt, **Paradise Bay** is further down the island and therefore a little more isolated, but if getting away from it all is what you want, then this is for you. It's basic, but it has a good, safe, shallow swimming beach. Development of the area has been hampered by the south-easterlies that sometimes rip through the place— it was wiped out by Cyclone Ada in early 1970.

ACCESS

The launch *Escape* departs Shute Harbour

every day at 9 a.m. for Palm Bay and Paradise Bay. Ring Contiki's Whitsunday Resort for information about transfers to their part of the world (079 469400 or 008 075125).

ACCOMMODATION

Palm Bay charges around $70 a night for a cabin that will fit six people. Otherwise, singles pay around $14 a night. Contact:

Palm Bay Resort
PMB 28
Mackay Queensland 4740
079 469233

Contiki's Whitsunday Resort charges $785 for seven nights full board with two adults sharing. Telephone 079 469400 or 008 075125.

Paradise Bay is having a refit. Contact Whitsunday Travel Centre (079 466255) to find out the latest.

CAMPING

Palm Bay supplies their own 'campotels', and charges $15 per person.

WALKING TRACKS

There are 13 km of graded walking tracks on Long Island maintained by the DCPW. A track heads south to Sandy Bay from Palm Bay and takes around one and a half hours there and back.

The northern track from Palm Bay passes through Contiki's Resort and leads to a lookout. The walk there and back takes about two hours.

There are no tracks leading out of Paradise Bay.

REGULAR SERVICES TO OTHER ISLANDS

A launch connects Contiki's Resort with Hamilton Island. The *Escape* will go anywhere anyone likes during the day.

NEAREST HELP

Shute Harbour..

The inexpensive cabins at Palm Bay, Long Island.

Hamilton Island

- **Resort**
- **Water**
- **Toilets**
- **Picnic area**
- **Fireplace**
- **Phone**
- **Walking tracks**
- **Suitable for disabled**

Hamilton Island has the appearance of being more of a town than a resort. It has its own supermarket and primary school.

The critics have variously described it as a real-estate venture with a resort on it, a fantasy village populated by smug, 'beautiful' people, even as an existentialist's nightmare. The brochures describe it as 'the most civilized tropical resort in the Pacific', or simply 'the best resort in the world'.

Hamilton Island is undeniably a resort of international standard serviced by a staff with a level of professionalism not often seen on other Queensland islands. But despite all the fun in the sun — soul, it has none.

It has a good sandy beach at the front of the resort when the tide's in. When the tide's out, there's a huge swimming pool for guests only.

Sit-down meals are expensive. Expect to pay $6 or more for a bowl of minestrone in the Pink Pizza Parlour, but only around $3 for a big chicken and salad sandwich from the Bakery. The Outrigger Room specializes in seafood, but not the local catch because commercial fishing is banned in the Whitsundays. The chef, Louis Pherhad, has worked in some of Melbourne's top restaurants. You pay top prices.

One of the features that the island likes to brag about is the Fauna Park, but the day I

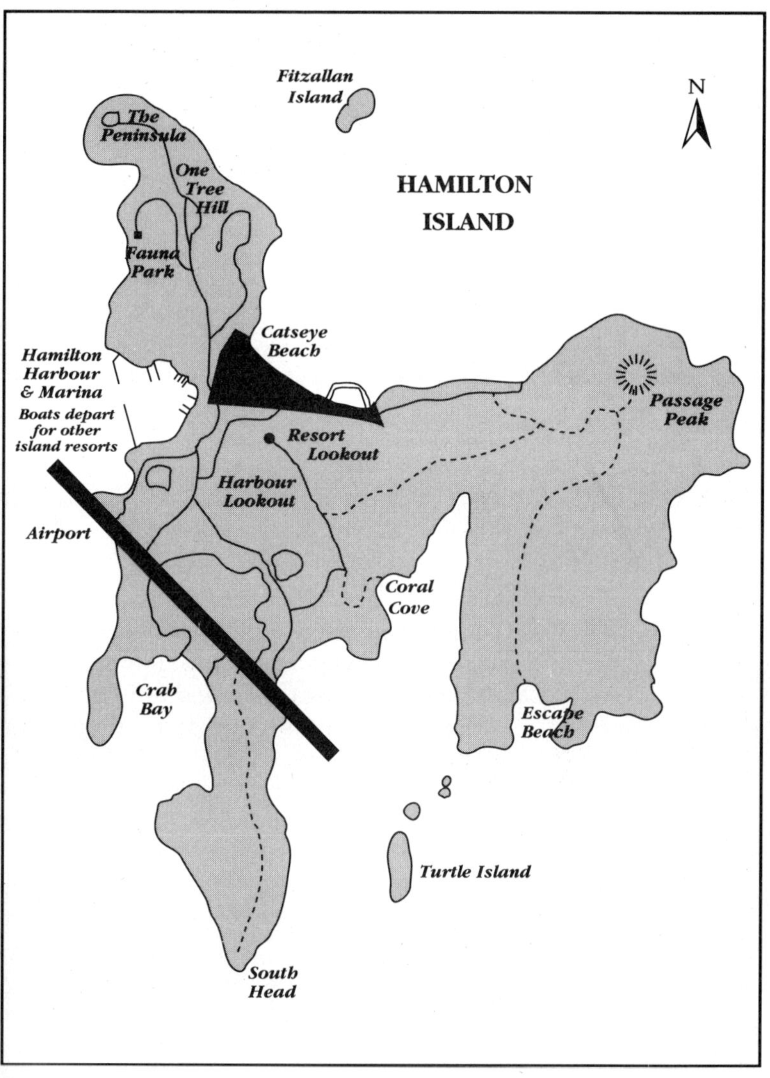
Fitzallan
Island
N
The
Peninsula
One
Tree
Hill
HAMILTON
ISLAND
Fauna
Park
Catseye
Beach
Hamilton
Harbour
& Marina
Boats depart
for other
island resorts
Passage
Peak
Resort
Lookout
Harbour
Lookout
Airport
Coral
Cove
Crab
Bay
Escape
Beach
Turtle Island
South
Head

was there the quokkas were hiding in a small and bare pen and the kangaroos didn't look like they were having a holiday in the sun at all.

Charter boats and buggies are obtainable at Hamilton Island Charters at the harbour (079 469144, ext. 8226/8227) or perhaps you might like to charter Australia's biggest speedboat belonging to the man behind the resort, Keith Williams. Over 20 metres long and capable of 45 knots, it's called *Awesome*.

That name just about sums up the resort itself.

Nearby **Dent Island** is about to be developed into Hamilton's golf course and health centre.

ACCESS

A launch, usually the *2000*, leaves Shute Harbour for Hamilton at 9 a.m. and 5.15 p.m. daily. The cost is around $25 return.

Hamilton has its own domestic airport with direct flights to Cairns, Townsville, Brisbane and other capitals. Light aircraft go to Mackay, Proserpine and Shute Harbour airports.

Day-trippers can get the 9 a.m. launch from Shute Harbour and use all the resort facilities except the swimming pools. The launch returns at 4.30 p.m.. There are picnic facilities in both the harbour and the resort areas.

ACCOMMODATION

Hamilton Island resort is unlike any other. It's a huge development with room for over 1000 guests. Add to this figure the few hundred people on their own boats in the harbour and a few more hundred in private flats, and you've got a whopping big resort.

Guests on Hamilton pay for their rooms only. There's a choice of eight restaurants or the suites have cooking facilities. For two adults sharing, the cost per week is:

Bures or Allamanda rooms	$700
Bougainvillea rooms	$840
One-bedroom suite	$927
Two-bedroom suite	$1225

There are cheaper ways of staying on Hamilton. There is a standby ratc available from $82.50 per night with two adults sharing, or if you were to fit five people into a Whitsunday Tower suite under the stand-by scheme, the cost would be a reasonable $52 a night each.

At the other end of the market, you could buy yourself a suite for $200 000, or perhaps a cruise on the luxury yacht *Achilles II* at $2000 a night for the stateroom.

The resort address is:
PMB
Mackay
Queensland 4740
079 469144 or 008 075110

WALKING TRACKS

The 2 km walk from the resort to Passage Peak and the short track down to Coral Cove from the vehicular track are steep in places. The island is a little over 500 hectares so most walks can be done comfortably in half a day.

REGULAR SERVICES TO OTHER ISLANDS

The *2000* goes to Whitehaven Beach on Whitsunday Island on Thursdays and Sundays and on to South Molle and Hook Islands on Tuesdays. The *War Canoe* runs across to an old couple's coral art shop on Dent Island three days a week.

NEAREST HELP

Hamilton Island has a resident doctor and nurses.

Gold Coast style buildings on Hamilton Island.

Whitsunday Island

Haslewood, Lupton, Border, Cid and Henning Islands

- **National Park (category C)**
- **Campground**
- **Bush camping**
- **Water**
- **Toilets**
- **Picnic area**
- **Fireplace**
- **Walking tracks**

W**hitsunday Island** is the biggest in the Whitsunday group. The whole island is national park and there is no permanent settlement on it. It's an ideal camping island.

In 1888, James Whitnall set up a sawmill at what is now called Sawmill Beach. He reported seeing aborigines. Sawmill Beach is now a favourite camping spot, with all facilities and freshwater tank. It is a sand beach with good anchorages. The headlands south of the beach are ideal for reef exploration.

There is a new walking track north of here to the camping area at **Dugong Inlet**. It also has a water tank and all facilities but the anchorage is shallow and access is only at high tide. There is a good beach with rainforest behind it. Shute Harbour is 20 km away and the nearest help is 14 km at Hamilton Island.

Whitehaven Beach is composed of fine white sand and is rated as the best beach in the Whitsundays. Situated on the south-eastern side of Whitsunday Island, the camping area is on the southern end of the 6 km beach and has facilities but no water. It is 35 km from Shute Harbour and the nearest settlement is 19 km away at Hook Island resort.

Other camping areas on the island are at **Scrub Hen Beach**, mainly used by commercial camping groups, and at **Nari's**

Whitsunday Island.

Beach and **Joe's Beach**. Day-cruise boats do drop-offs to these spots but neither has good anchorages.

Take insect repellent to Whitsunday Island!

Haslewood Island

Lupton Island

Some of the islands surrounding Whitsunday have good camping areas too. **Haslewood Island**, to the east, has camping areas on Chalkie's Beach and Windy Bay. **Chalkie's Beach** has no facilities and water only in summer. **Windy Bay** is close to the reef that separates Haslewood from **Lupton Island**, which is ideal for walking and exploration. It's 34 km from Shute Harbour and 19 km from Hamilton Island, the nearest civilization.

Border Island

To the north of Haslewood is **Border Island**. There are good sites here on **Cateran Bay**, but there is no water and no facilities. Shute Harbour is 35 km and Hook Island Resort is 10 km away.

Cid Island

Closer to Shute Harbour (13 km) and on the west side of Whitsunday is **Cid Island**. There are campsites at **Homestead Bay** on the west side of the island. Nearest help is 8 km away at South Molle. No water or facilities.

Henning Island

South of Cid Island is jungle-clad **Henning Island**. There are two camping areas at the **North Spit**, which has facilities, and at **Geographer's Beach** on the west side, with no facilities. Neither has water. Shute Harbour is 16 km to the west and Hamilton Island 5 km to the south-east.

Shute Island

Shute Island is so close to Shute Harbour you could almost swim across. Being as close as it is to the Whitsunday's boating hub, it's not your get-away-from-it-all island, but it sure is handy.

There are campsites on the north-west beach with all facilities but no water.

Tancred Island and Repair Island

Tancred and **Repair Islands** are between Shute Harbour and the slightly larger Shute Island. Tancred has a few secluded sites on the northern part of the island with no facilities and no water. Repair is a day-visit island with no campsites. The three islands are surrounded by coral.

- **National Park (category C)**
- **Campground**
- **Toilets**
- **Picnic area**
- **Fireplace**

South Molle Island

South Molle Island is a 490 hectare national park with a resort on it. The resort was virtually wiped out in January 1970 by Cyclone Ada — Daydream and Hayman Islands were hard hit too and thirteen people died as a result of this cyclone.

Run by Ansett, which also runs the very up-market Hayman resort, South Molle is a casual family resort.

As with many other Whitsunday resort beaches, the beach here is made of coral rubble and is affected by tidal changes. At low tide it can smell like a sewage farm.

South Molle resort is notable for having a lounge the size of an aircraft hangar and a small golf course. The resort area is quite busy when the day visitors arrive. There are moorings available for visiting yachtspeople.

North Molle Island, Planton and Denman Islands

- **National Park (category C)**
- **Resort**
- **Water**
- **Toilets**
- **Picnic area**
- **Fireplace**
- **Phone**
- **Walking tracks**
- **Suitable for disabled**

North Molle Island

North Molle Island is a national park with two campgrounds. The ten sites in the north-west at Hannah Point are on a coral beach, and Cockatoo Beach on the southern end has 15 sites, and is sandy at high tide. About 10 km from Shute Harbour, both have facilities and water, but neither has good anchorages. It's possible to walk along the coast between the two.

Planton and Denman Islands

Off the eastern shore of South Molle are **Planton** and **Denman Islands**. There are a few sites on each, but no water, facilities or good anchorages.

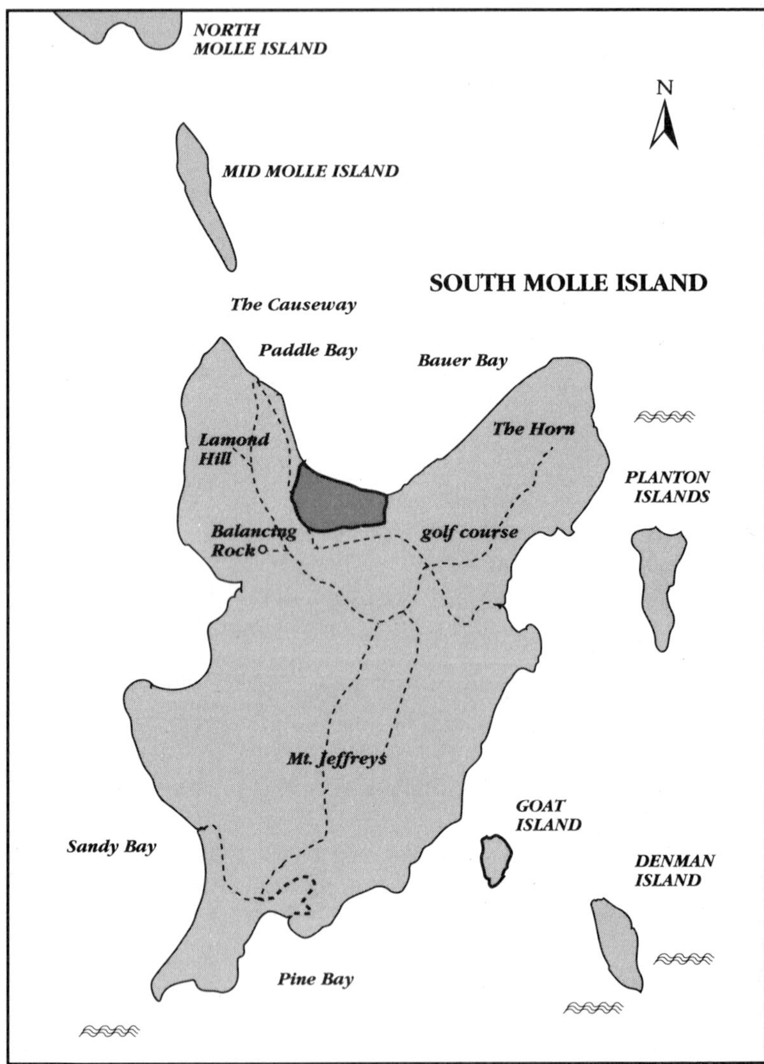
NORTH
MOLLE ISLAND
N
MID MOLLE ISLAND
SOUTH MOLLE ISLAND
The Causeway
Paddle Bay
Bauer Bay
The Horn
Lamond
Hill
PLANTON
ISLANDS
Balancing
Rock
golf course
Mt. Jeffreys
GOAT
ISLAND
Sandy Bay
DENMAN
ISLAND
Pine Bay

ACCESS

A launch leaves Shute Harbour at various times daily for South Molle. The cost is $20 return. Check with the resort for other departures.

Day-trippers can use all resort facilities and there is a picnic area for their use.

ACCOMMODATION

South Molle is a family resort aimed at the middle of the market. It has over 200 rooms, some on Bauer Bay, some on the golf course and others that just look onto other rooms.

For two adults sharing for a week, the cost of the Golf Reef, Golf Family or Polynesian units is $735, the Beachside Reef or Beachcomber $875, and the Whitsunday units $980. There is a standby rate of $65 per person a night.

Contact the Resort:
PMB 21
Mackay Queensland 4741
079 469433 or 008 075080.

or the Mainland Reservations Office:
South Molle Travel Centre
43 Shute Harbour Road
Airlie Beach.
Queensland 4802
079 466900

WALKING TRACKS

South Molle Island is covered by walking tracks, all maintained by the DCPW.

Follow the foreshore footpath of the resort to the west to get to the start of the tracks that lead to Paddle Bay (0.5 km) and Lamond Hill (2 km).

The tracks going to the eastern and southern parts of the island begin behind the golf course. The longest walk, to Sandy Bay and Pine Bay, is 4 km.. Mt Jeffreys is 2.2 km and to the east Oyster Bay is 1.2 km away and Spion Kop or The Horn is 2.2 km. Tracks marked on the map are approximate.

Middle Molle and North Molle Islands as seen from South Molle Island.

REGULAR SERVICES TO OTHER ISLANDS

The big resort catamarans *The Capricorn* and *The Reef* go to several of the Whitsunday islands during the week.

There is a daily trip to Hook Island leaving the South Molle Island resort at 9.30 a.m.. It costs $28 for guests of the resort and $38 for non-guests. It's called the Hook Island/Nara Inlet Cruise.

On Fridays a boat goes to Hamilton Island at 1.45 p.m. and at 9.30 a.m on Sundays and Thursdays there's a trip to Whitehaven Beach on Whitsunday Island and the observatory on Hook Island. It costs $35 for guests and $40 for non-guests.

NEAREST HELP

The resort has a nurse, or Shute Harbour (8 km).

Daydream Island

- **Resort**
- **Water**
- **Toilets**
- **Phone**
- **Walking tracks**
- **Suitable for disabled**

Daydream, or West Molle Island, will be closed until late 1990 for a total renovation. A new resort is to be built on the north end of the island and the old one at the southern end bulldozed and turned into a day-trippers' area. It will remain an all-inclusive resort pitched at the middle of the market.

Bought by Reg Ansett along with Hayman in 1948, Daydream is now run by the owners of Sea World on the Gold Coast.

The island has three coral beaches. There are moorings but they're not very good.

ACCESS
The launch will continue to leave Shute Harbour for Daydream several times a day.

ACCOMMODATION
Contact the resort by writing to:

Daydream Island Resort
via Proserpine
Queensland 4800
079 469200 or 02 2515469

WALKING TRACKS
A track dissects the island from the old resort to Sunlovers Beach. Well-formed but rough, it's about a 3 km round trip. Sunlovers Beach is popular with day cruise yachts.

NEAREST HELP
Shute Harbour (6 km)

Hook Island

- **National Park (category C)**
- **Resort**
- **Campground**
- **Bush camping**
- **Water**
- **Toilets**
- **Picnic area**
- **Fireplace**
- **Walking tracks**

Hook Island is the next biggest island in the Whitsunday group after Whitsunday Island. Like Whitsunday, it's a rugged, rocky, mountainous island covered in forest. There are three coral beaches. It has one small resort on the strait that separates Hook Island from Whitsunday. The rest of the island is national park.

Hook resort is a popular spot for day visitors because it is the base for such things as the underwater observatory and coral-viewing water craft. But before 11 a.m. and after 2 p.m. the resort area can be very quiet. Accommodation is in basic cabins or tents (your own).

The resort has the appearance of a scout camp at jamboree time, with its flags from different countries out the front. The clientele is mostly the younger camping crowd. Meals are supplied and there is a refrigerator for guest use. There is a bar and store, which stocks milk, bread and some expensive fruit and vegetables. Best to BYO.

The resort doesn't have a public phone. Some moorings are available. Take insect repellent because sandflies can be a problem.

See under Camping for details about DCPW-maintained campsites on other parts of the island.

ACCESS

The *Gypsy* or the *Princess* leaves Shute

Harbour at 8.15 a.m. each morning. The cost is $15.

South Molle's Hook Island/Nara Inlet Cruise leaves Shute Harbour for Hook Island at 9 a.m. each morning. There is ample time for people to tour the underwater observatory (well worth it), view the coral from the Whitsunday Coral Sub (there's a marine biologist on board to answer questions) and have lunch (the food is ordinary). The cost is $38 return.

Australian Regional offers a seaplane service to the island.

ACCOMMODATION

There are 12 basic bunk-style cabins at the resort that house eight people each. They cost $15 a night for a bed.

There are meals available — dinner and lunch cost about $10. Otherwise, there are cooking facilities for guests.

Bookings and enquiries can be made at the South Molle Travel Centre (079 466900) or South Molle Resort (079 469433). The resort is run by Ansett Airlines, which also runs South Molle.

The resort's address is:
PMB 23
Mackay
Queensland 4741

It's possible to ring by dialling South Molle resort and asking for extension 521.

CAMPING

There are around 20 campsites in two small camping areas on both sides of the resort. The cost is $7.50 per person per night.

Butterfly Bay, on the west side, has 12 sites with no facilities and water only in summer. It is 34 km from Shute Harbour, and Hayman Island is the nearest outpost of civilization (8 km).

Nara Inlet is known as one of the best anchorages in the Whitsundays. The DCPW and the Army have completed a boardwalk to caves with Aboriginal drawings. Check with the DCPW about campsites in the area.

Curlew Beach in Macona Inlet, **Stonehaven** and **Butterfly Bay East** have small camping areas with no facilities or water.

Scuba diving off Hook Island.

WALKING TRACKS

Pebble Beach is a beautiful spot with sweeping views up the eastern side of the island. To get to it, walk up the four-wheel drive track behind the resort towards the generator. Signs indicate a steep walking track up the hill to the right and down to the beach. It should take around 15 minutes.

A short track runs south to the underwater observatory. Another track heads north through the camping area, into the forest and down to the rocks. This is an alternative way to Pebble Beach.

REGULAR SERVICES TO OTHER ISLANDS

The day-visitor boats do regular trips between Hook Island resort, South Molle Island and Hamilton Island.

NEAREST HELP

South Molle resort nurse.

Butterfly Bay Beach, Hook Island.

Hayman Island and Langford Island

- **Resort**
- **Water**
- **Toilets**
- **Phone**
- **Walking tracks**

Hayman Island is Australia's most up-market island resort. It has undergone a $300 million renovation, and the island is virtually 'locked-up' unless you're a paying guest. Dubbed 'Beyond 2000' by the locals, there were extensive delays in getting the work finished. The 'building experiments' have added millions to the original estimated $140 million bill.

The father of Ansett Airlines, Reg Ansett, bought the lease on Hayman in 1947 for £10,000. He established the first resort in 1950 with the idea of creating more traffic for his airline in the slack winter months.

With over 200 rooms it can accommodate 500 guests. To give you an idea of the cost of the new resort, diners can expect to pay over $100 each to eat at the best resort restaurant, La Fontaine. There has been no expense spared in the refit: the big date-palms were transported from a convent in Swan Hill, Victoria; the swimming pool is the size of five Olympic pools; the toilet taps are gold-plated; and so on.

Langford Island

Hayman has some of the best fringing coral in the Whitsundays. Nearby **Langford Island** has an extensive reef popular with the day-cruise boats. Or the resort dive boat *Reef Goddess* does trips out to the Hardy/Black/Hook reef complex on the Great Barrier Reef. Hayman is the closest of the Whitsunday Islands to this reef.

ACCESS

The resort boats *Sun Goddess* and *Sun Paradise* pick up guests from Hamilton Island airport. Or there's the helicopter service from Hamilton Island to Airlie Beach.

ACCOMMODATION

Rooms on Hayman can cost anything from $255 to over $1500 a night for a penthouse suite. Meals are extra.

Ring the resort on 079 469100 or 008 251657 and work out a deal.

WALKING TRACKS

The 400-hectare island has a 2 km walk to Blue Pearl Bay on its western side.

Dolphin Point, the northern tip of the island, is 3.5 km and the circuit walk back along the rugged northern shoreline is 8 km long.

REGULAR SERVICES TO OTHER ISLANDS

The *Sun Goddess* and *Sun Paradise* connect Hayman with Hamilton Island.

NEAREST HELP

The resort has its own ambulance service. Shute Harbour is 30 km away.

The Tropical North Islands

The islands of the tropical north are either continental, such as Lizard Island in the far north, or coral cays, such as Green Island off Cairns. The continental islands are generally surrounded by fringing reefs.

The main centres are Townsville and Cairns.

Townsville is the site of Great Barrier Reef Wonderland, which houses the world's biggest artificial coral reef, complete with a transparent tunnel running through it. For those who want to experience the real thing, Pro-dive, in the same building, run diving courses. Mike Bell, next to Civic House, has another dive shop and diving instruction school.

John Brewer Reef has its own floating hotel called, oddly enough, the Floating

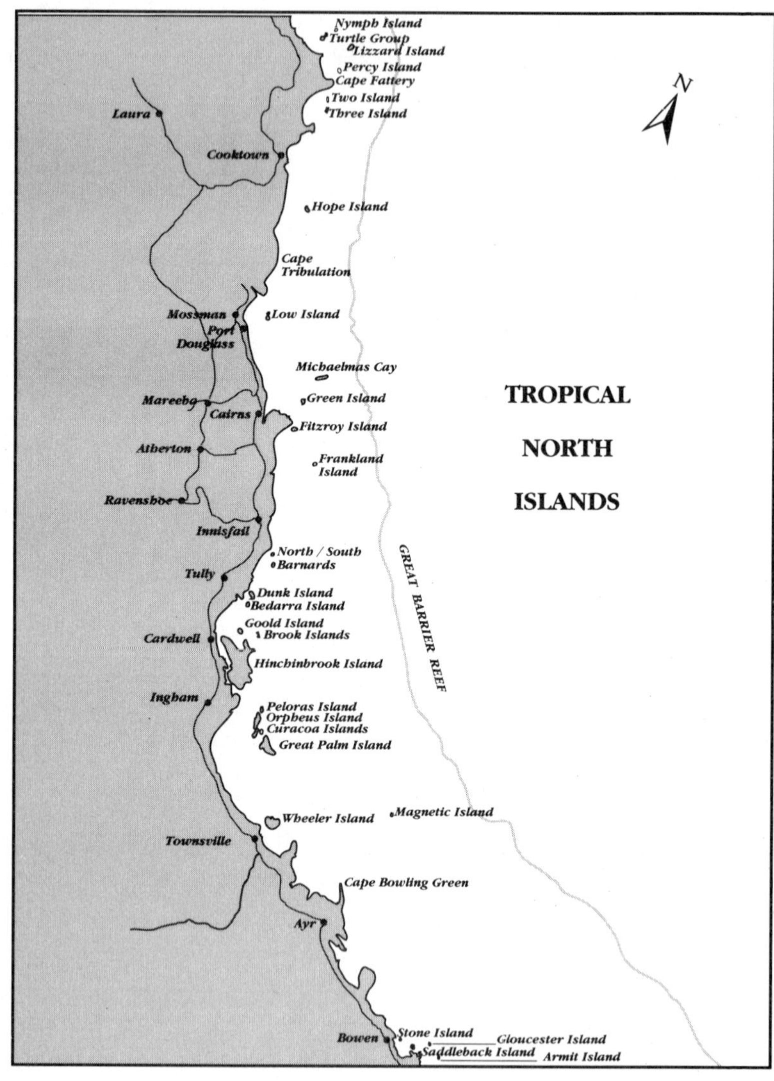
Nymph Island
Turtle Group
Lizzard Island
Percy Island
Cape Fattery
Two Island
Three Island
Laura
Cooktown
Hope Island
Cape Tribulation
Mossman
Port Douglass
Low Island
Michaelmas Cay
Mareeba
Green Island
Cairns
Fitzroy Island
Atherton
Frankland Island
Ravenshoe
Innisfail
North / South Barnards
Tully
Dunk Island
Bedarra Island
Goold Island
Brook Islands
Cardwell
Hinchinbrook Island
Ingham
Peloras Island
Orpheus Island
Curacoa Islands
Great Palm Island
GREAT BARRIER REEF
Wheeler Island
Magnetic Island
Townsville
Cape Bowling Green
Ayr
Bowen
Stone Island
Gloucester Island
Saddleback Island
Armit Island
N
TROPICAL NORTH ISLANDS

Hotel. The 400-bed hotel was built in Singapore and towed to its present site. Their telephone number is 077 709111.

The Reef Travel Centre (077 724688) has lists of dive and charter boats.

Further up the coast, the Great Barrier Reef Dive-inn in the Mission Beach Hub Shopping Centre has scuba courses for full certification for $250. Introductory courses cost $50. Ring 070 687294.

Cairns is the tourist hub of the north. It now has an international airport. Old houses on stilts have been flattened to make way for new international hotels, and the once quiet Esplanade along the foreshore is now like a back street in Kings Cross.

Cairns has ample diving facilities. Down Under Aquatics (070 551724) and Going Places (070 514055) take divers out to the Outer Reef. Pro-dive (070 519915) go to the Reef and have diving courses as well.

There are several regular passenger boat services to the Outer Reef. See under entries for Fitzroy and Green Islands, Michaelmas Cay and the Low Isles.

Contact the Far North Queensland Promotions Bureau in Cairns (070 513588) for information about charter boats, helicopter and aircraft services to the Great Barrier Reef.

Gloucester Island

Saddleback, Eshelby and Armit Islands

- **National Park (category C)**
- **Campground**
- **Bush camping**
- **Toilets**
- **Picnic area**
- **Fireplace**

Gloucester Island, and some of the islands around it, are national park camping islands. **Gloucester**, the largest island of the group, has 15 campsites with toilets, fireplace and picnic area at Bona Bay, on the north-west side. The island is home to the Proserpine rock wallaby. There is no water supplied. Nearest help is at Monte's Resort, 3 km on the other side of the passage that separates the island from the mainland. Access is via Dingo Beach (12 km) or Bowen.

Saddleback Island

Closer to Dingo Beach is **Saddleback Island**. There are 15 sites on the north-west point. None has water but they do have facilities. There have been reports of death adders on the island.

Eshelby Island

Eshelby Island, to the north-east of Saddleback, doesn't have a camping area but has a good beach and lots of birdlife.

Armit Island

Armit Island has 15 sites at West Beach. There are toilets and fireplace but no water. Access is via Earlando (10 km) or Airlie Beach (20 km).

Dingo Beach and Earlando on the mainland are reached by a dirt road that runs off the back road to Airlie Beach. Dingo Beach has a general store and some units and Earlando has a general store and camping area.

CLOSEST DCPW OFFICE
Whitsunday Office
PO Box 332
Airlie Beach
Queensland 4802
079 469430

The Forts, an old World War II signal station on Magnetic Island.

Stone Island

- **Resort**
- **Campground**
- **Water**
- **Toilets**
- **Picnic area**
- **Fireplace**
- **Phone**

There is a small low-key resort on Stone Island, which is close to the historic town of Bowen. Bowen was founded in 1861, two years after the Moreton Bay district of New South Wales became the colony of Queensland. Bowen was the first port and the capital of Northern Queensland at a time when most of it had yet to be explored.

Stone Island is surrounded by beaches and the resort has a swimming pool. Its proximity to Bowen makes it popular with the locals on weekends. Don't expect a get-away-from-it-all tropical paradise - the island didn't get its name for nothing.

You can hire canoes, catamarans and mokes at the resort.

ACCESS

Ring the resort (077 861101) to arrange to be picked up by the Island launch in Bowen.

ACCOMMODATION

There are seven units for $30 per person per night. The resort can accommodate 45 people. Their postal address is:

PO Box 902
Bowen, Queensland 4805
077 861101

NEAREST HELP

Bowen.

Magnetic Island

- **National Park**
- **Resort**
- **Campground**
- **Water**
- **Toilets**
- **Picnic area**
- **Fireplace**
- **Phone**
- **Ranger staff**
- **Walking tracks**
- **Suitable for disabled**
- **YHA**

M**agnetic Island** has some good things going for it: a choice of cheap accommodation, cheap and easy access and great beaches. Like Great Keppel Island, it's popular with the budget traveller.

Magnetic is a granite-based continental island covered in eucalypt woodland. It's so close to Townsville that its towns of Picnic Bay, Nelly Bay, Arcadia and Horseshoe Bay are virtually suburbs, but what suburbs!

The size of the island is 5184 hectares and about half is national park.

Picnic Bay is the main town and the most used destination for the ferry. It has a mall with shops, post office and a great little eating place at one end called Maggie's.

There have been no large-scale tourist developments as yet, but **Nelly Bay** is the site for a proposed marina.

Arcadia has the best hostel (see Accommodation) and the best hotel. There are minimal *après plage* offerings on the island, but a lot of them happen here.

There is a post office at the shopping centre.

At the end of the road, about 10 k m from Picnic Bay, is **Horseshoe Bay**, the island's biggest beach and site of the only campground (Geoff's Place). To drive to the end of Horseshoe Bay, turn off the main road down Gifford Street and follow this road around to the right.

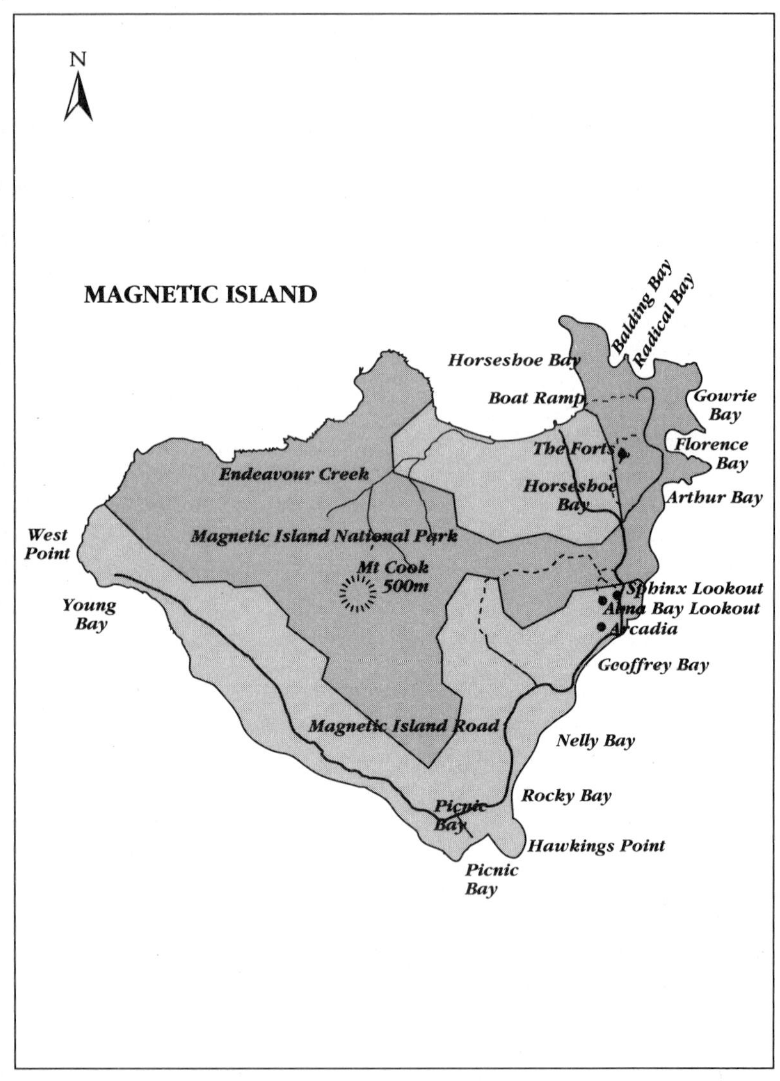
N
MAGNETIC ISLAND
Balding Bay
Radical Bay
Horseshoe Bay
Boat Ramp
Gowrie Bay
The Forts
Florence Bay
Horseshoe Bay
Arthur Bay
Endeavour Creek
West Point
Magnetic Island National Park
Mt Cook 500m
Sphinx Lookout
Alma Bay Lookout
Arcadia
Young Bay
Geoffrey Bay
Magnetic Island Road
Nelly Bay
Rocky Bay
Picnic Bay
Hawkings Point
Picnic Bay

Magnetic Island has prolific birdlife with over 160 species recorded. There's the eerie-sounding bush stone curlew, the giant wedge-tailed eagle and the spectacular rainbow bird. Other colourfully named species include the spangled drongo, mongolian dotterel, boobook owl, bar-tailed godwit, brown booby and helmeted friarbird. The common sparrow, crow and magpie are also present.

The woodland is mostly eucalypt such as bloodwood, stringybark, grey ironbark and white-barked poplar gum. Hoop pine grows along the coast.

Movement around the island is by bus (077 785130), taxi (077 785484), motorbike or bicycle (077 785222, 077 785544), moke (077 785703, 077 785491, 077 785377) or hitchhiking. Mokes cost around $20 a day. There are restrictions on where they can go and such as along the dirt road to West Point. It's easy to get bogged in sand on the 8 km road! It's not recommended as a walking track either, being flat and uninteresting; but Young Bay, at walk's end, is a pleasant enough beach.

Diving courses and gear are available at Magnetic Diving, Shop 4, in the Arcadia Shopping Complex (077 785799). They have one day 'resort' courses for $50 and open-water diving courses for $265. There is a maximum of eight people in each class, so individual attention is assured.

Sea-wasps can be a problem between October and April.

ACCESS

The Magnetic Marine ferry departs from the Magnetic Marine wharf at 168 Flinders Street in Townsville, just down from the GPO. The cost is about $10 return. It goes to Picnic Bay or Arcadia several times a day. Ring 077 772122 for details.

The Magnetic Marine car ferry leaves from Ross Street, on the other side of the river from the passenger terminal. It only goes to Arcadia. Ring 077 716737 for costs and times. Passengers on the car barge pay $4 return.

Westmark Ferry Services operate a regular passenger service to Picnic Bay. The cost is the same as the Magnetic Marine ferry. Ring them in Townsville on 077 211913 or on the island on 077 785374.

ACCOMMODATION

There's plenty to choose from on Magnetic Island.

The best hostel-type places are Centaur House in Arcadia and 80 Picnic Street in Picnic Bay.

Centaur House has bunkrooms and one big room with single beds. It overlooks Geoffrey Bay (which doesn't have a very good beach) with Cape Cleveland and Mt Elliot in the distance. There is a wonderful shady sitting area out the back.

The address for Centaur House is:
27 Marine Parade
Arcadia
Queensland
077 785668.

80 Picnic Street is a clean and comfortable place with 16 beds in five rooms. It's popular so it's best to book in advance. A track leads from the end of Picnic Street to a great little beach at Rocky Bay. They have a courtesy car (077 785755).

Geoff's Place is a busy little place on Horseshoe Bay. It's the biggest 'hostel' on Magnetic Island and the only place you can pitch a tent. It's close to good beaches and walks.

The cabins are fairly run-down and the atmosphere is like a college kids' summer camp but they have good food. Their number is 077 785577.

The **Queensland Recreation Council** runs a **recreation camp** at Picnic Bay which is affiliated with YHA. It's spartan, and the dormitories are cramped, but if you don't mind the youth-camp feel of the place, it's cheap. YHA members pay around $5. The number is 077 785280.

Backpackers Headquarters at Picnic Bay is plain and has small rooms. But it's adequate. Their number is 077 785110.

Expect to pay around $8 per night for any of the backpacker accommodation.

Magnetic Island has two resorts worth a mention. The **Latitude 19 Resort** in Nelly Bay costs $360 a week for two adults sharing in their Lodge rooms or $665 for the Executive Suites. Their number is 077 785200.

The **Radical Bay Resort** (077 785294), has standard units or Bungalows.

The **Magnetic Island Tourist Association** has a complete list of places to stay at, available from tourist information centres and travel agents.

CAMPING

Geoff's Place at Horseshoe Bay has grounds set aside for camping and some established tents. Ring 077 785577 for prices.

WALKING TRACKS

The walk from **Nelly Bay to Arcadia** starts at the end of Mandalay Avenue. It's a 6 km, 2 hour walk. At the saddle about halfway between the two towns, it's possible to follow the ridge westwards up to the summit of Mt Cook. This is an 8 km all-day walk. Bad fires have been through here recently and the terrain is showing the scars.

The track up to the **forts** is well worthwhile. It begins at the Horseshoe Bay Road and Radical Bay Road intersection, and is the old access road to the forts. The walk takes about 45 minutes. The forts were built in 1942 for the Army in the event of a Japanese invasion. From here you can walk down a steep track to **Florence Bay. Radical Bay** is another 1 km up the sealed road. This road is a 'semi-private' one to the resort but is open to the public. There's a bar and refreshments available.

Another good track runs from **Radical Bay to Horseshoe Bay**. It takes about an hour. The turnoff to Balding Bay from the Radical Bay/Horseshoe Bay track is about halfway. The beach is good and there is a picnic area. The descent to Horseshoe Bay from the turnoff is steep, rough and rocky. It comes out at the eastern end of Horseshoe Bay beach.

A less arduous track runs from the road connecting Picnic Bay and Nelly Bay to Rocky Bay beach. This is another top beach. The distance is only 500 metres or so.

CLOSEST DCPW OFFICE

The Ranger
Hurst Street
Picnic Bay Queensland
077 785378

or: Northern Regional Centre
Marlow Street,
Pallarenda
PO Box 5391
Townsville Mail Centre
Queensland 4810
077 741411

The Northern Regional Centre is out of town and difficult to get to unless you've got a car.

NEAREST HELP
Magnetic Island Ambulance (077 793722)

Radical Bay Beach, Magnetic Island.

Orpheus Island

Great Palm, Fantome, Curacoa and Pelorus Islands

- **National Park (category C)**
- **Resort**
- **Campground**
- **Bush camping**
- **Toilets**
- **Picnic area**
- **Phone**
- **Walking tracks**

Orpheus Island has one of the more exclusive resorts on the Queensland coast. It has camping areas too but because of its distance from the coast, about 24 km, it's expensive to get to.

The resort is small and intimate with room for about 50 guests. Children under 12 aren't allowed, there's no TV and only one telephone line. Day-trippers and yachties are not permitted by the management — the same company runs the Sebel Town House in Sydney and the Windsor in Melbourne. There's no entertainment either, so it's not really a resort for the young or young at heart. Guests are encouraged to take a picnic hamper on an outboard dinghy and disappear for the day to one of several isolated beaches.

It's a peaceful place, the still of the night interrupted only by the whirr of the spa motor, and there's great attention to detail, such as a small collection of dried flowers left on a turned sheet of the bed after dinner.

The island is a narrow strip about 11 km long with an area of 1368 hectares. It's an ideal island for snorkelling around some of the fringing reefs. The beaches are generally exposed at low tide.

I left the island, rather reluctantly, just before a volleyball match between staff and guests on the beach. Somewhere between Orpheus and Lucinda on the power cat called *The Black Jack* there's a sudden stop, and 400 hp of outboard motors are turned off because the skipper can't hear a radio message from the resort. 'Do you know where the volleyball pump is?...(crackle, crackle)...over,' comes the request. The skipper replies 'No, Bowie knows where it is, but he's out windsurfing...over.' 'Thanks Paul, over and out.'. It's a hard life.

Great Palm, Fantome and Curacoa Islands

The Palm Islands, **Great Palm, Fantome** and **Curacoa**, are controlled by an Aboriginal community and it is necessary to get permission from the Palm Island manager if you want to land. These islands are directly south-east of Orpheus.

Pelorus Island

Immediately north of Orpheus is **Pelorus Island**. This is uncommitted crown land.

ACCESS

There is a seaplane service from Townsville for $182 return. Jim Judge runs the water taxi *Scuba-do* from Dungeness, near Lucinda, from around $200 a day.

Pure Pleasure Cruises has a daily service from Townsville. It costs $70 and is basically a day-tripper/diving service. Ring 077 888322 for more details.

ACCOMMODATION

For two adults sharing, the resort on Orpheus Island charges $1960 a week for its

Studio rooms and $2240 for the bungalows. All meals are included.

The address of the resort is:
PMB
Ingham
Queensland 4850
077 777377 or 008 221837

CAMPING

There are camping areas on Orpheus Island at **Pioneer Bay**, north of the resort, and at **Yank's Jetty** on **Yankee Bay**, south of the resort. Both have toilets and tables but no water. Yank`s Jetty was the site of a ship demagnetizing works during World War II. They did this to repel mines.

Category C fees are payable to DCPW Offices in Ingham or Townsville.

Orpheus Resort and a fisherman's tall story.

WALKING TRACKS

There's a 15 minute walk to **Horseshoe Bay** behind the resort. Follow the car track that leads up past the private units to a saddle and walk down from here.

There's also a track from the resort to **Picnic Bay** which takes about 40 minutes.

CLOSEST DCPW OFFICE

Hinchinbrook District Office
PO Box 1293
Ingham
Queensland 4850
077 761700

or: Northern Regional Centre
PO Box 5391
Townsville Mail Centre
Queensland 4810
077 741411

NEAREST HELP

The resort and the James Cook University research station at Pioneer Bay have telephones.

Hinchin-brook Island

Goold, Garden and The Brook Islands

- **National Park (categories B and C)**
- **Resort**
- **Campground**
- **Bush camping**
- **Water**
- **Toilets**
- **Picnic area**
- **Fireplace**
- **Phone**
- **Walking tracks**

Hinchinbrook Island is the best island on the Queensland coast for bushwalking and camping. At 39 000 hectares it is Australia's and possibly the world's biggest island national park.

It is an island of unspoilt wilderness. The rugged peaks, with Mt Bowen at the top (at 1142 m it is Queensland's third highest mountain) gives way to steep rainforest and mangrove flats to the west and steep and undulating rainforest or scrub to the east. Only the east coast has beaches.

The mangrove forests on the west side and in **Missionary Bay** are some of the most extensive in Queensland. There are 23 species of mangrove tree known to be present. The Australian Institute of Marine Science has a research station on Missionary Bay devoted to finding out more about them. The mangroves build land for themselves by collecting silt and organic material.

Most of the launches that leave Cardwell, a well-serviced but quiet little town on the mainland and Hinchinbrook's best access point, visit the AIMS research station, as well as the camping areas of Scraggy Point and Macushla (see under Camping), the resort at Cape Richards and Ramsay Bay.

Ramsay Bay is the starting point for the wilderness trek down to Zoe Bay, a popular walk with experienced bushwalkers (see under Walking Tracks). The boats weave

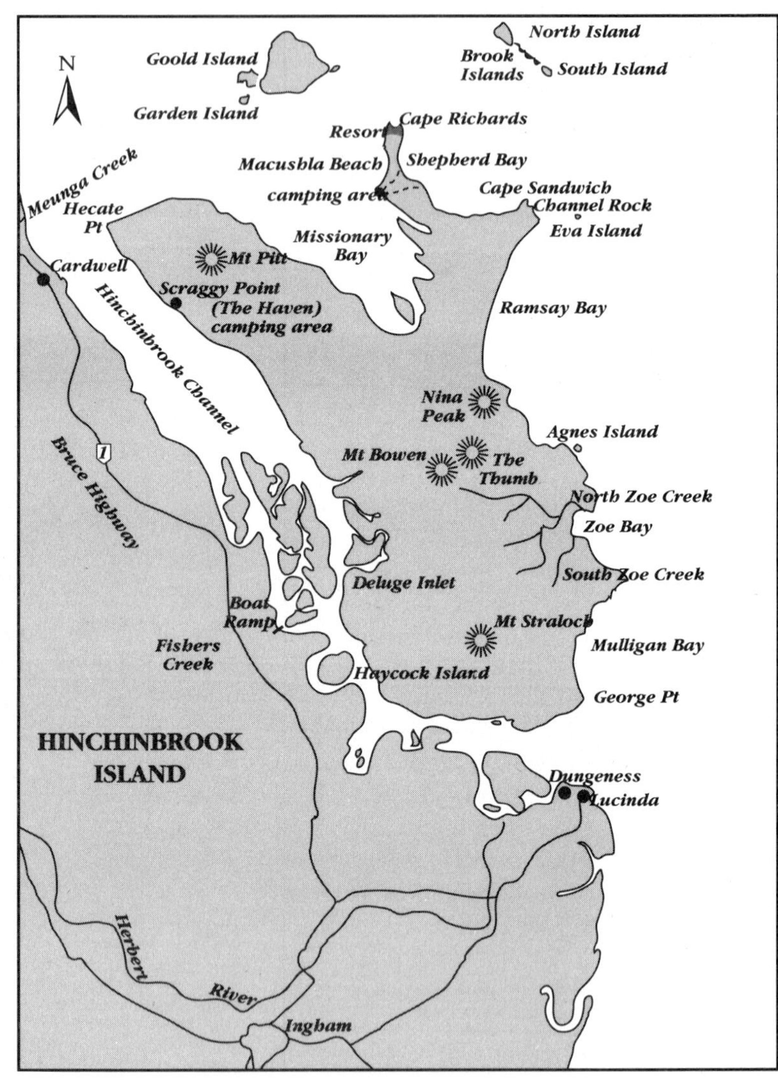
N
Goold Island
Garden Island
North Island
Brook Islands
South Island
Cape Richards
Resort
Macushla Beach
Shepherd Bay
Meunga Creek
Hecate Pt
camping area
Cape Sandwich
Channel Rock
Eva Island
Missionary Bay
Mt Pitt
Cardwell
Scraggy Point (The Haven) camping area
Ramsay Bay
Hinchinbrook Channel
Nina Peak
Agnes Island
Mt Bowen
The Thumb
Bruce Highway
1
North Zoe Creek
Zoe Bay
South Zoe Creek
Deluge Inlet
Boat Ramp
Mt Straloch
Fishers Creek
Mulligan Bay
Haycock Island
George Pt
HINCHINBROOK ISLAND
Dungeness
Lucinda
Herbert
River
Ingham

their way through narrow waterways in the mangrove forest in Missionary Bay to get to it. It has a good shallow beach and the massif of Mt Bowen rising from the south end. The bay is well known locally for the flotsam that washes up on the beach — Japanese liquor bottles are highly prized.

Insect repellent is a must if you're camping as biting insects are bad, particularly in or near the mangroves.

Marine-stingers are present between November and March and saltwater crocodiles inhabit the waterways. Do remember to take all litter out.

The new office of the DCPW in Cardwell is the place to go for information about walking, camping or just visiting the island. The rangers are very helpful and permits for camping are available here.

Topographical maps (Cardwell, 1:100 000) and marine maps are available from Cardwell Travel Agency (070 668661).

There are two other islands in the area that are ideal for camping.

Goold Island

Goold Island, a national park, has campsites on a good sand beach on its western side. There are pit toilets, fireplaces and tables but water in summer only in a creek at the northern end of the beach. It is necessary to walk through water from the boat to get to the beach so it is best to minimize on gear. Walking through the forest is easy.

The explorer Edmund Kennedy stopped at the island in 1848 in the *Tam O'Shanter* on his way to a mainland beach just north of here. The party landed there because the area had been described as having 'low wooded hills' when in fact they were covered in rainforest. From here he began his ill-fated trek up to Cape York where he was speared to death by Aboriginies.

Garden Island

Garden Island is a small council controlled-recreation reserve. There are no restrictions on camping or pets. There's a good sand beach but no water.

Brook Islands

The **Brook Islands** have a day-visitor area on a beach on the north-west side of **North Island**. Hinchinbrook Island resort guests often come out here. Camping is banned because the islands are an important breeding ground for the pure white Torres Strait pigeon.

ACCESS

Access to Hinchinbrook, and the other islands, is mostly by launch from Cardwell.

The Cardwell Travel Agency operates the *Tekin.* This boat runs to the resort and as far afield as Orpheus and Dunk Islands. Contact them on 070 668661.

Hinchinbrook Island Booking Office has the *Hinchinbrook Explorer* which also goes to the resort, Macushla, the AIMS walk and

Ramsay Bay, and the *Reef Venture* which runs to the resort every day except Monday for $30 return. For an extra $15 you can stay as a day guest and have lunch. See them also about houseboats. Telephone 070 668539.

There are two boat services that approach the island from the south. The *Searcher* goes to Deluge Inlet and Scraggy Point from Lucinda for $25. They have started a service to George Point to enable walkers to walk up to Zoe Bay and on to Ramsay Bay. Contact them on 077 778307 for details.

Seair Pacific Airlines flies to the resort from Townsville for around $200 return.

ACCOMMODATION

There is a small resort on Hinchinbrook Island at Cape Richards, built in the old Queensland colonial style. It has self-contained units in the bush, away from the simple but cosy bar and dining room.

The resort sits on an excellent sand beach. 'A million miles from the nearest disco', there is no entertainment supplied. There is a small store for guests only.

For two adults sharing, a half-cabin costs $945 a week and a full cabin $1155, full board. There is a standby rate of $80 per day.

Contact them by writing to:

PO Box 3
Cardwell
Queensland 4816
070 668585.

CAMPING

Macushla and **Scraggy Point** are the two camping areas on Hinchinbrook Island with facilities. Both have toilets, tables and fireplaces but only Scraggy Point has water. Containers for water can be borrowed from the boat operators. There is space for 35 people and a maximum stay of seven days is imposed on each campground (as on Gould Island). Macushla has a category B fee and the rest a category C.

Macushla has the advantage of having walking tracks to South and North Shepherd Bays and the resort. Meals are available for campers at the resort if they are in small numbers and well dressed.

The closest place to hire camping equipment is Wongaling Hire at Mission Beach on the mainland.

WALKING TRACKS

A 2 km track runs from **Macushla** to the southern end of **North Shepherd Bay**. There is a sign to Shepherd Bay halfway along the beach on the northern side of the point at Macushla. About 1 km along this track through coastal forest is a turnoff to South Shepherd Bay. There is a 2 km graded walking track through rainforest from the north end of North Shepherd Bay beach to the resort. The walk from Macushla to the resort takes around 2 hours.

A more challenging walk is from **Ramsay**

Bay to **Zoe Bay**. There is no formed track but rather a fairly well-defined trail tagged with orange triangles and the occasional red plastic strip. The 12 km walk takes a full day but allow four days for the return trip if you're thinking of taking it at a leisurely pace.

The trail begins at the southern end of Ramsay Bay and leads to Blacksand Beach after 1 km. Nina Bay is another 2 km, followed by Little Ramsay Bay (2.5 km), Banksia Bay (2 km), North Zoe Creek (5 km), and South Zoe Creek (3 km).

Water is available only at Nina Bay, Little Ramsay Bay and South Zoe Creek, so it is suggested that you carry enough water to see you through the first stage to Nina Bay.

Best campsites are at **Blacksand Beach, Nina Bay, Little Ramsay Bay,** and **South Zoe Creek.**

It is necessary to wade across North Zoe Creek at low tide to get to Zoe Bay Beach. Even at low tide it can be over a metre deep. A crossing should not be attempted in deep water because of the danger of saltwater crocodiles. There is a track up South Zoe Creek to a permanent waterfall. There are usually yachts anchored at Zoe Bay.

A new trail leads from **Zoe Bay south to Mulligans Bay/George Point** where *The Searcher* lands (see under Access). It's reasonably rugged and takes about 4 hours.

It is possible to walk up **Mt Bowen** from

Little Ramsay Bay by following the gorge. This is advised only for the experienced bushwalker; allow two days to reach the summit. There are no tags and it can be very steep and rough in places. The descent to Zoe Bay is by following North Zoe creek or Warrawilla Creek.

Get the DCPW Information Sheet *Coastal Walks* for more information.

CLOSEST DCPW OFFICE

There are two offices in the area. Cardwell has a big new information centre with its own rainforest display. The office at Ingham can be used by people approaching the island from the south.

Cardwell Office
Bruce Highway
PO Box 74
Cardwell Queensland 4816
070 668601

Hinchinbrook District Office
2 Herbert Street
PO Box 1293
Ingham Queensland 4850
077 761700

NEAREST HELP

Cardwell or the resort

Dunk Island

- **National Park**
- **Resort**
- **Campground**
- **Water**
- **Toilets**
- **Picnic area**
- **Fireplace**
- **Phone**
- **Walking tracks**
- **Suitable for disabled**

Dunk Island is one of the few islands in Queensland actually covered in lush tropical rainforest. It receives a high rainfall because of its closeness to Queensland's highest mountains: Mt Bowen on Hinchinbrook Island to the south and Mt Bartle Frere, Queensland's highest at 1612 m, to the north. The town of Tully, not far from Dunk Island, gets 3700 mm of rain a year. Dunk Island is the largest, the 'father' in the Family group of islands. It's about 75 percent national park, with the remainder divided up between resort, a farm and an artists' 'colony'. Two artists from the Eltham district of Victoria live here and sell their works to visiting tourists.

It is thought that 400 Aborigines lived on the island before Edmund Banfield arrived to live here in the late 1890s. They were reportedly expert at bark-canoe manufacture. The coastline of Dunk, along with other Family islands, has she-oaks, paperbarks, Moreton Bay ash and patches of pandanus palm and mangrove. Inland there are the big swamp mahogany, bloodwoods, red stringy - bark and strangler figs, along with Alexandra and fan palms and the annoying 'wait-a-while' vines.

The island was struck by Cyclone Winifred in 1986, but though winds of 220 km/h ravaged the rainforest, the mainland seems to have been worst hit.

N
DUNK ISLAND
Purtaboi Island
Kartee Point
Muggy Muggy
Mt Kootaloo 271m
Brammo Bay Resort
jetty
golf course
The Spit camping area
Pallon Beach
Airstrip
dairy
walking tracks
farm
Palm Valley
National Park
clay target shooting
Bruce Arthurs Place
Coconut Beach

The resort's capacity for 300 guests and 150 staff, with day visitors and camper activity by the jetty, makes Dunk Island a busy place but it's not hard to get away from it all on the many walking tracks.

Marine stingers are present between November and March.

ACCESS

Most people, at least most of the day visitors, get a launch from Clump Point at North Mission Beach on the mainland. There are several to choose from.

The *Quick Cat* is the fastest and goes to Dunk Island daily for $18 or Beaver Cay on the Great Barrier Reef for $78. The trip out to the cay takes about 60 minutes from Dunk Island. Phone 070 687289 for more details.

The *Friendship* runs every day except Mondays. It costs $12 to Dunk and $28 for a cruise around the other Family Islands (includes lunch). The *Friendship Flyer* costs $48 to Beaver Cay. Their number is 070 687245.

The *Lawrence Kavanagh* costs $12 to Dunk. An extra $8 will give you lunch in the day-visitor area on the island. It costs another $4 for a cruise past Bedarra Island. Ring 070 687211.

Water taxis do the trip in 10 minutes or so. The *Kyamera* leaves Wongaling Beach five times a day. It costs $14 and the number there is 070 688310. The fastest trip of them all is the *Cassowary* that leaves opposite 120 Kennedy Esplanade at South Mission Beach five times a day and also costs $14. Their number is 070 688333.

The luxury cruise boat *Coral Princess* visits Dunk on its four-day cruise between Townsville and Cairns. Ring 070 514066 for details.

There are regular Australian Regional flights to Dunk Island airstrip from Cairns and Townsville.

ACCOMMODATION

A resort on Dunk Island was first established in 1934 from the bungalow that was the home of Dunk's famous beachcomber and author, Edmund Banfield.

Today the resort, now owned by Australian Airlines, can accommodate 300 guests in 150 rooms. The cost for each person for two adults sharing for a week is $1007 for the Banfield rooms, $1176 for the Garden Cabana rooms and $1414 for the Beachfront suites. There is one room suitable for the disabled. The resort's phone number is 070 688199.

CAMPING

The camping area on Dunk Island is presently under the control of the DCPW but there is talk of handing it over to the resort. With sites for about 30 people, it's advisable to book in advance. Just ring the Cardwell

DCPW and ask for a permit number. The DCPW ranger residence at Mission Beach is out of the way and hard to find.

The campground has good facilities with a shower and toilet block, water, fireplaces and tables. Three days is the maximum stay allowed. There is a kiosk and bar which is shared with the day visitors. It's open from 9 a.m. to 5 p.m. most days, staying open later on Friday and Sunday nights. A can of beer is not cheap, but they supply ice for those with an esky.

Although the resort has 'Resort area - Guests Only' signs everywhere, campers and day trippers can visit the resort during the day, but not after 6 p.m.

WALKING TRACKS

There are 13 km of walking tracks through Dunk's tropical rainforests and to secluded sandy beaches.

The biggest walk is to **Mt Kootaloo via Coconut Beach**. It's about a 5 hour round trip back to the resort so it's best done as a leisurely day-walk. Don't expect panoramic views from the summit, but it's nice enough. Alternatively, you can scale Mt Kootaloo from the resort in 2 hours.

Coconut Beach takes about an hour to get to and there are freshwater streams on the way where you can top up water bottles. The tapestry weaver Bruce Arthur has his home just off the Coconut Beach track and it takes about 40 minutes to reach it..

A shorter track to **Muggy Muggy Beach and Kartee Point** is found by following the signs from the resort to Banfield's grave. The beach is pebbly but swimming is possible at high tide.

CLOSEST DCPW OFFICE

Cardwell Office
PO Box 74
Cardwell
Queensland 4816
070 668601

NEAREST HELP

The resort's first-aid clinic

The campground on Dunk Island.

Bedarra Island

Wheeler, Coombe and Bowden Islands

- National Park (category C)
- Resort
- Bush camping
- Water
- Toilets
- Picnic area
- Phone
- Walking tracks

Bedarra Island, the 'mother' of the Family Islands, has the distinction of being one of the most expensive island resorts in Australia. There are two exclusive resorts, both aimed squarely at the luxury market. Campers, day-visitors, and even children are banned. The manager claims that the freehold title to the island extends to the low-water mark, which means a fisherman who steps out of his boat on to the reef could technically be fined for trespassing. He didn't say whether anyone had actually been caught.

The two resorts have been developed quite recently by their owner, Australian Airlines. The artist and conservationist John Busst built the Plantation homestead, now **Bedarra Bay resort**, in 1942. **Hideaway resort** was just a collection of cabins as recently as 1984.

The artist Noel Wood has owned a small block of land on one corner of the island since 1936.

The island is blessed with four sandy beaches but one thing the tourist advertising doesn't mention is the presence of death adders, stonefish and, of course, marine stingers between November and March.

Five of the Family Islands near Bedarra are national parks. **Timana Island**, between Bedarra and Dunk, is privately owned.

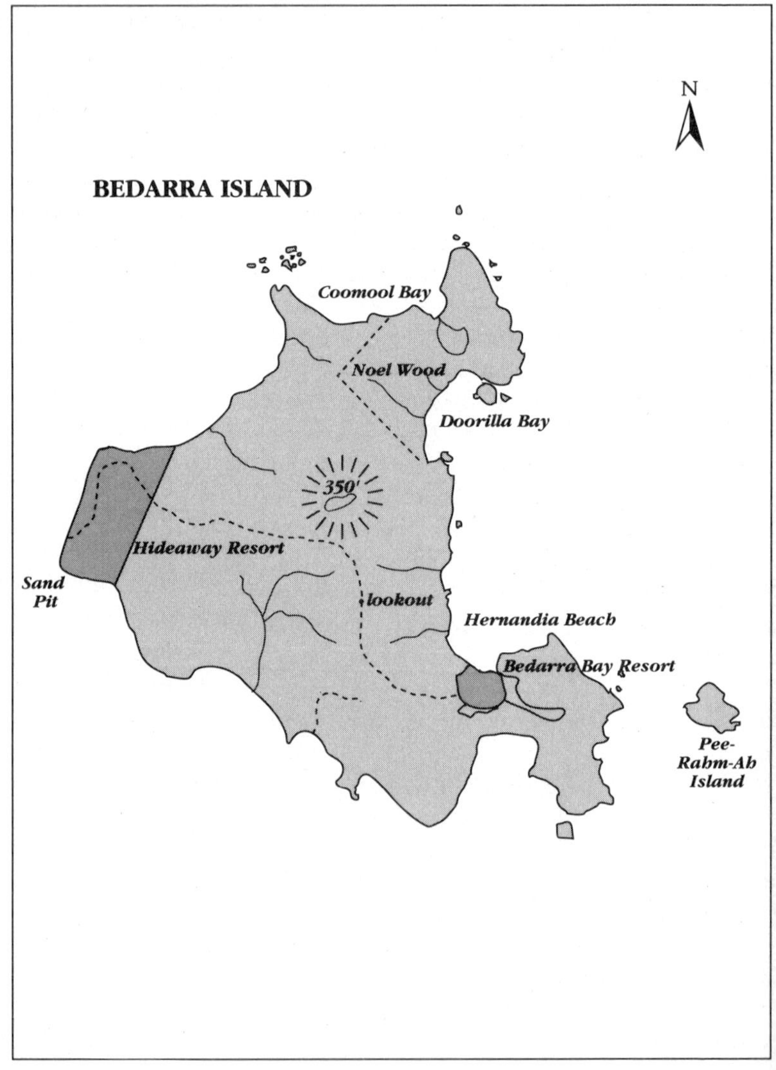
N
BEDARRA ISLAND
Coomool Bay
Noel Wood
Doorilla Bay
350'
Hideaway Resort
Sand
Pit
lookout
Hernandia Beach
Bedarra Bay Resort
Pee-
Rahm-Ah
Island

Wheeler, Coombe and Bowden Islands

Three of the national park islands are suitable for camping — **Wheeler, Coombe** and **Bowden.** Wheeler and Coombe have some good beaches. There are sandspits on the north-west side of all the national park islands. It's necessary to take in water and cookers and there is a maximum stay of seven days. There are no allocated sites so bush camping is the order of the day.

The *Friendship* can do drop-offs to Wheeler. It leaves from Clump Point at Mission Beach on the mainland and their number is 070 687245. Otherwise, there's the Mission Beach water taxis, but they're expensive, or local charter boats.

ACCESS

By launch from Dunk Island. It's free for guests.

ACCOMMODATION

Both resorts on Bedarra cost $3115 each for two adults for one week. There is room for only around 30 guests in each resort, housed in 16 private villas. Bedarra Bay's number is 070 688233 and Hideaway's 070 688168.

WALKING TRACKS

There is a single walking track which dissects Bedarra Island between the two resorts. The island is small, only 80 hectares, and is covered in tropical rainforest: coast walking can be difficult and rough.

CLOSEST DCPW OFFICE
Cardwell
PO Box 74
Cardwell,
Queensland 4816.
070 668601.

NEAREST HELP
Dunk Island

What tourists' dreams are made of (Dunk Island)

South and North Barnards

- **National Park (category C)**
- **Bush camping**

The Barnards are an out-of-the-way group of islands between Mission Beach and Innisfail. Camping is permitted on **Stephens Island** in the South Barnards and **Hutchison Island** in the North Barnards.

Stephens Island has space for 15 people on the west end of the island. At Hutchison there is space for 10 people on the north-west side. A maximum stay of 14 days applies to both. Access is by private boat or water taxi.

Permits are available from the closest DCPW office at 88 Rankin Street in Innisfail or the Cairns office.

Frankland Islands

- **National Park (category C)**
- **Bush camping**

These islands consist of four national parks. Camping is permitted on **Normanby Island**, the northernmost of the group, and **High Island.** Each site is located on the north-west side of the island and there is space for 15 people. Fourteen days is the longest you can stay.

The high-speed catamaran *Banyandah* does regular runs out to the Franklands from Deeral landing, near the mouth of the Mulgrave River. They pick people up in Cairns at 8 a.m. and drive them down to Deeral. Contact 070 554966.

The budget accommadation on Fitzroy Island.

Fitzroy Island

Fitzroy Island is a hilly forest- covered island specializing in budget accommodation, and is an easy boat ride away from Cairns. It's highly recommended for its walks, coral-viewing and value for money.

Frequented mostly by backpackers, locals, divers, families and the odd tour, it's quiet (there's no airport) and has some good beaches. The main beach in front of the resort is made of broken coral and is most suitable for snorkelling but **Nudey Beach** is made of sand and, yes, people have been known to take their clothes off there.

Welcome Bay is the only anchorage on the island. Visiting boats can use the jetty by the resort after 4.30 p.m. There is a water-tap on the jetty.

Welcome Bay was well known last century as a place to get water and as a good anchorage amongst the beche-de-mer fishermen. Beche-de-mer, or sea slugs, were destined for the Chinese gourmet market.

There is a dive centre on the island. Peter Boundy Dive Centre has courses in scuba diving ranging from introductions for $50 to five day courses for $290. This includes accommodation. Their number is 070 510294.

The resort hires out catamarans and canoes.

- **Resort**
- **Campground**
- **Water**
- **Toilets**
- **Picnic area**
- **Fireplace**
- **Phone**
- **Walking tracks**

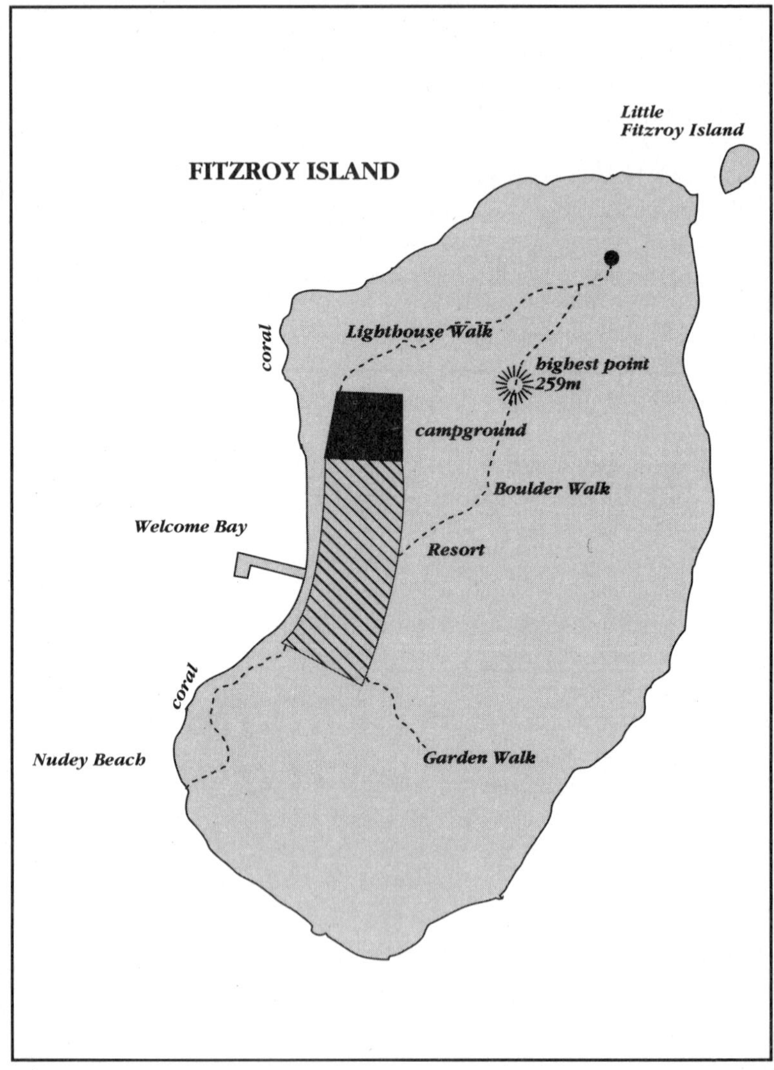
FITZROY ISLAND
Little
Fitzroy Island
coral
Lighthouse Walk
highest point
259m
campground
Boulder Walk
Welcome Bay
Resort
coral
Nudey Beach
Garden Walk

The island has something of a rubbish problem. There are two big tips that I saw — one beside the camping area and another off the road to the lighthouse. Perhaps the resort should consider cutting down on disposables, such as plastic knives and forks.

ACCESS

Great Adventures Cruises runs the *Fitzroy Flyer* across to Fitzroy from Cairns in 45 minutes. It costs $28 return.

The *Reef Adventure* goes out to Moore Reef, in good conditions, for $66 return. Ring Great Adventures on 070 510455 for more details.

The *Reef Runner* goes to Fitzroy and the Outer Reef for $39. Ring 070 510444.

ACCOMMODATION

Fitzroy Island resort is classy, but without all the hype of some of its bigger brothers down south. And it's reasonably cheap. If you are prepared to share a four -bunk room, it's $24 a day. Sheets are supplied. There is a communal kitchen, too. If you want a room to yourself, that will cost $595 for a week. The villas have meals included except lunch and they cost $105 a day per person sharing. The resort has a restaurant and bar, a laundry, a kiosk, a grill and a small supermarket.

The resort's address is:
PO Box 2120
Cairns
Queensland 4870
070 519588

CAMPING

There are about 20 sites at the council campground next to the resort — the resort manages the campground. It has toilets, showers, tables and fireplaces. Permits are needed and you can get them from the Great Adventures office in Wharf Street in Cairns. The cost is $10 a day per site. Maximum stay is four weeks.

WALKING TRACKS

Fitzroy Island offers some terrific walks. The best is the combined **Lighthouse and Boulder Walk**. Take the vehicle track out of the resort to the lighthouse. This is very steep in places, but the lighthouse is well worth a look. Another steep car track runs up to an old World War II gunnery. From here there's a narrow walking track to the summit of the island's biggest hill.

There are no signs around the big boulders at the peak to identify the track back down to the resort but it's roughly on the opposite side of the peak from where the track comes up from the lighthouse. It's a steep and rugged decline to the resort — in fact, it's not so much a walk as a climb down. You'll pass a 1000-year-old zamia palm on the track near the resort.

If the Boulder and Lighthouse walks are done separately they will each take about one and a half hours for the return trip. It's an hour return to Nudey Beach and the Garden walk takes half an hour return.

REGULAR SERVICES TO OTHER ISLANDS

Great Adventures Cruises have regular services to Green Island (see Access for contact numbers).

CLOSEST DCPW OFFICE

Northern Regional Office
41 The Esplanade
PO Box 2066
Cairns
Queensland 4870
070 519811

NEAREST HELP

Cairns Base Hospital (070 506333).

Green Island

- **National Park**
- **Resort**
- **Water**
- **Toilets**
- **Picnic area**
- **Phone**
- **Walking tracks**
- **Suitable for disabled**

Green Island is probably the busiest island off the Queensland coast. It's a tourist mecca because of its closeness to Cairns, its tourist facilities, its beaches and the fact that it's a true coral cay. At 12 hectares, it's very small and you do get the feeling you're on an island, though it can get pretty crowded.

There are 30 units attached to the resort but most people visit the island for the day. It has almost an amusement-park quality — a place for the family and the tourist. It's a popular dive spot too and has its own dive shop.

Beche-de-mer fishermen used to camp on the island at the end of the last century. In 1873, the *Goodwill* landed with Aboriginal men and women: the fishermen insisted that the women stay ashore with them while the men remained aboard. The Aboriginal men revolted, not surprisingly, and killed two of the white men. Daniel Kelly escaped by rowing to Oyster Cay. He returned to find the *Goodwill* gone.

Hayles, now Great Adventures, started cruises to the island in 1928 — every two weeks! They established the first glass-bottomed boats in Queensland at Green Island in 1937, the year the island became a national park. The underwater observatory was built in 1954. 500 hectares of reef surrounding the cay were declared a marine park in 1974.

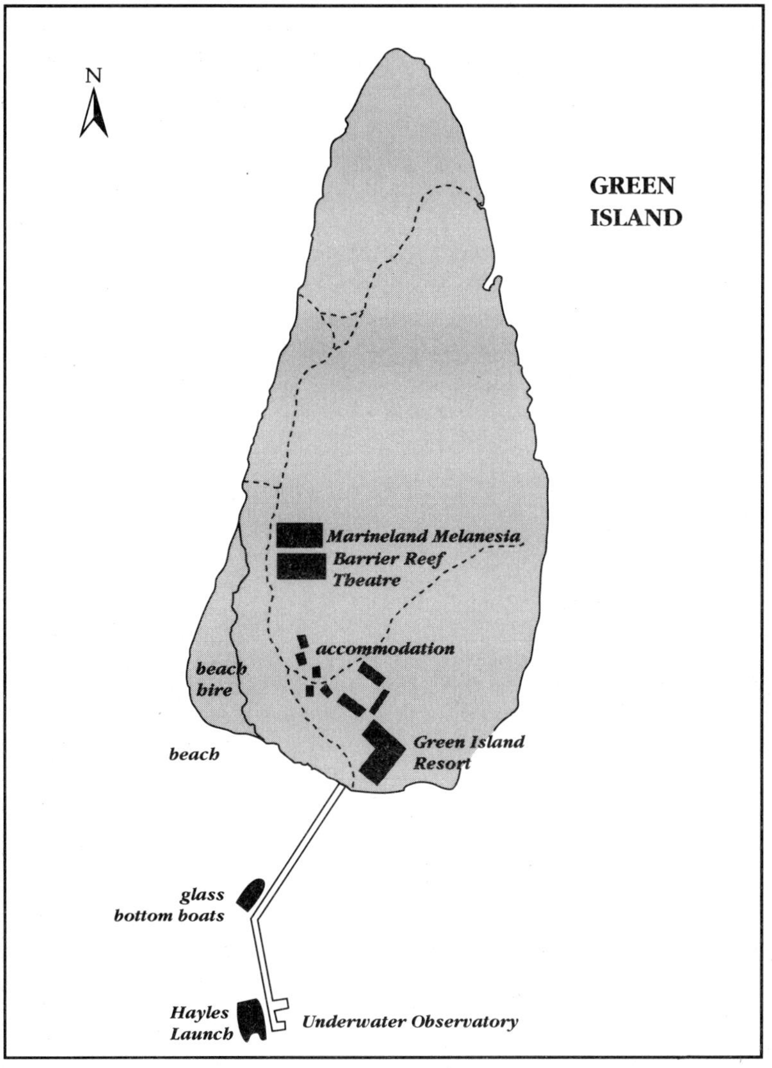
N
GREEN
ISLAND
Marineland Melanesia
Barrier Reef
Theatre
accommodation
beach
hire
beach
Green Island
Resort
glass
bottom boats
Hayles
Launch
Underwater Observatory

Crocodiles can be seen at Marineland Melanesia.

The Barrier Reef Theatre is a small cinema screening films about the history of the island and the reef by the husband-and wife-diving team, Rod and Valerie Taylor.

Marineland Melanesia is an odd mixture of New Guinean art and marine life. They have 'Cassius' on display — at about 6 m, the largest captive saltwater crocodile in Australia. You might have trouble seeing him because most of his bulk is under water. There are other crocs of various ages on view too.

The buffet lunch meals are similar in style and price to those on Fitzroy Island.

There are moorings for small boats and the jetty can be used when not being used by the cruise boats.

ACCESS

Great Adventures has catamarans that do the trip in 40 minutes for $33 return. The budget launch takes one and a half hours but costs only $20 return. Great Adventures also goes out to Norman Reef ($95 return), Michaelmas Cay ($76 return) and Fitzroy Island ($42 return). Ring 070 510455 for departure times.

Big Cat Tour Services uses the *Big Cat* to Green Island for $20. Dolphin Dive, aboard the *Big Cat*, have introductory scuba courses for $45.

Ring 070 510444 for more information.

ACCOMMODATION

The Palm units cost $691 each for two adults sharing for a week, and the Tropical units $770. Enquire about standby rates by ringing the resort on 070 514644.

REGULAR SERVICES TO OTHER ISLANDS

Great Adventures services Fitzroy Island and Michaelmas Cay (see under Access).

CLOSEST DCPW OFFICE

Northern Regional Office
41 The Esplanade
PO Box 2066
Cairns Queensland 4870
070 519811

NEAREST HELP

Cairns Base Hospital (070 506333).

Michaelmas Cay

• **National Park**

M**ichaelmas Cay** is a tiny coral island formed by coral sand 40 km north-east of Cairns. It's part of the Great Barrier Reef. Popular with day-cruise boats, the island is an important area for ground-nesting sea birds. There are over 14 species, including the sooty tern which can still breed in its 30th year. The island is national park and surrounded by marine park. There is access only to the sandy beach on the northern side. The bird-nesting area can be observed from here.

Great Adventures does a daily trip from the Great Adventures jetty in Wharf Street, Cairns, via Green Island, for $76 return, leaving at 8.30 a.m.. Or the *Ocean Spirit* catamaran leaves Marlin Marina at 8.30 a.m. every day for $89 return. Their number is 070 312920.

Low Isles

The **Low Isles** are low indeed — only 2m above sea-level at their highest point.

A lighthouse built in 1878 sits on a small, sandy cay overlooking a larger mangrove covered island. The sand cay is favoured by day cruise boats. There's good snorkelling and swimming off the beach and it's a good anchorage.

The *Reef Express* leaves Port Douglas daily at 10 a.m. for the 20-minute trip. The cost is $45 from Port Douglas or $55 from Cairns.

Contact:

Quicksilver/Low Isles Cruises
The Marina Mirage
Port Douglas
Queensland 4871
070 995500

or telephopne Cairns Tour Services (070 518311) for details.

The same company operates the 'Quicksilver' service to Agincourt Reef on the Outer Barrier Reef.

Snapper Island

- **National Park (category C)**
- **Campground**
- **Picnic area**
- **Fireplace**

Snapper Island, a national park, lies just off Cape Kimberley, not far from the mouth of the Daintree River.

A continental island, as distinct from other islands in the area such as the Low Isles which are coral cays, it nevertheless has fringing coral reefs.

A camping area sits on the north-west point. It has fireplaces and tables. The best beach, made of fine coral rubble, is here. There are 40 sites and there's a maximum stay of 14 days. See the Cairns office of the DCPW for a permit.

Snapper Island Cruises operates a daily service from Port Douglas for $35. Their coach does pick-ups in Cairns. Ring 070 311552 for details.

Hope Islands

- **National Park (category C)**
- **Bush camping**

The Hope Islands are two small islands about 10 km north-east of Cedar Bay.

East Hope Island has a camping area on its east side with ten spaces and a maximum stay of 14 days. It is fringed by good beaches. **West Hope Island** is covered in mangroves.

Access is by private boat — there's good anchorage on the north-west side of East Hope. Both islands are surrounded by extensive reefs.

See Cairns DCPW for permits.

Lizard Island

Three Islands, Two Islands, Rocky Islets, Turtle Group and Nymph Island

- **National Park (categories B and C)**
- **Resort**
- **Campground**
- **Water**
- **Toilets**
- **Picnic area**
- **Fireplace**
- **Phone**
- **Walking tracks**

Lizard Island has a lot to brag about: 23 beaches, great coral, undisturbed clear seawater, over 1000 hectares of national park to explore and one of the best anchorages off the coast.

Most people seem to associate Lizard Island with the expensive resort on its western side — which won the National Tourism Award for Best Resort of the Year in 1986 — but Lizard also has a campground and some good walks.

The island is ideal for snorkelling and the resort specializes in scuba diving, with its own introductory course, and big-game fishing. It's only 15 km from the Outer Reef.

The national park was established in 1939. In 1987 it was extended to include the surrounding islands of **Palfrey, South, Bird** and **Osprey**, and **Eagle Island**.

Land birds seen on Lizard Island include the sunbird, dollar bird, Torres Strait pigeon and the fabulous rainbow bird.

The island is well known for a tragedy in 1891, when Mary Watson set sail in a beche-de-mer boiling tub to escape hostile Aborigines. While Captain Watson was out to sea in search of the delicacy, Aborigines attacked their home, killing a Chinese servant. Another Chinese servant, plus Mary Watson and her young child, fled and were found on nearby Howick Island, dead from thirst. Apparently they were attacked

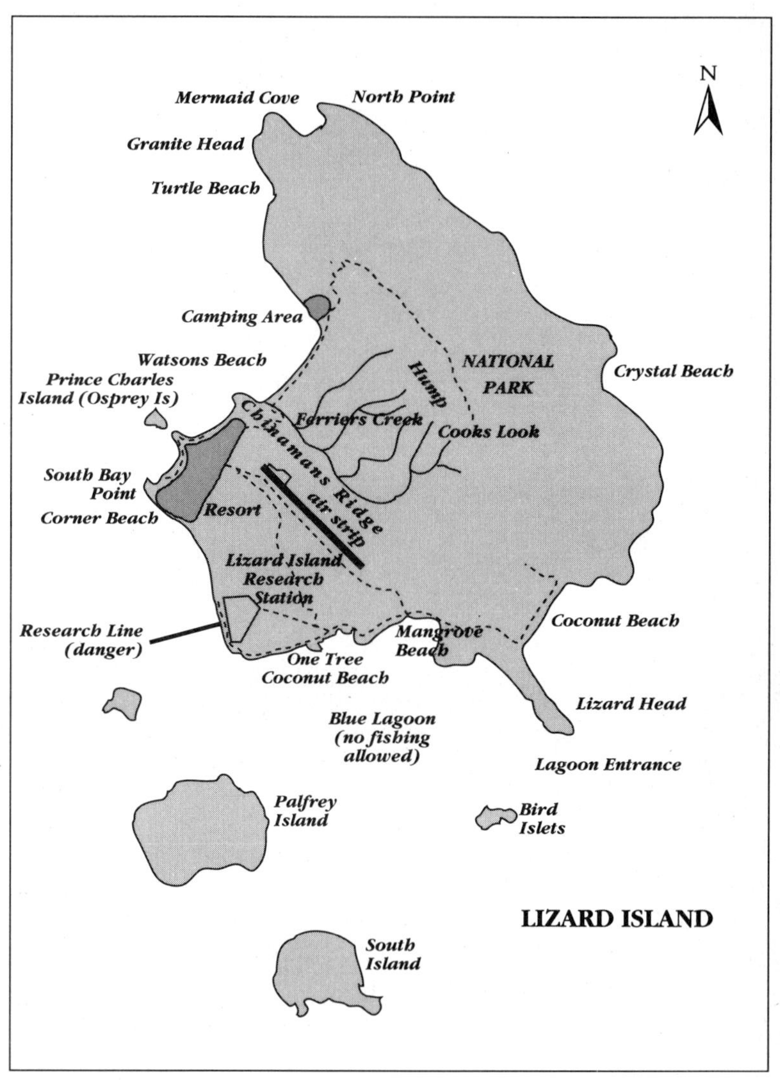
N
Mermaid Cove
North Point
Granite Head
Turtle Beach
Camping Area
Watsons Beach
Prince Charles
Island (Osprey Is)
NATIONAL
PARK
Crystal Beach
Hump
Chinamans Ridge
Ferriers Creek
Cooks Look
South Bay
Point
Corner Beach
Resort
air strip
Lizard Island
Research
Station
Research Line
(danger)
Mangrove
Beach
Coconut Beach
One Tree
Coconut Beach
Lizard Head
Blue Lagoon
(no fishing
allowed)
Lagoon Entrance
Palfrey
Island
Bird
Islets
LIZARD ISLAND
South
Island

because they were on sacred ground where women were strictly forbidden. The remains of their house is at the southern end of **Watsons Beach**.

Watsons Bay is the safest anchorage on the island, particularly in strong trade-wind conditions.

There are several national park islands between Lizard Island and the mainland that are suitable for camping.

Three Islands

About 40 km north-west of Cooktown are **Three Islands**. Camping is permitted on the south-west side of the largest one in the group. There is space for 20 people.

Two Islands

Just 10 km north of Three Islands are **Two Islands**. Up to 20 people are permitted to camp on the western tip of the larger island.

Rocky Islets

To the north again are the **Rocky Islets**. The largest island in the group is a continental island surrounded by a large reef. Thirty people can camp on the north side of this island between February and September only.

Turtle Group

To the west of Lizard Island is the **Turtle Group**. Here there are six coral cays mostly covered in mangroves. Camping is allowed on three of them.

Nymph Island

Just to the north-east of the Turtle Group is grass-covered **Nymph Island**. A maximum of 30 people are permitted to camp on any part of the island.

All of the islands have 14-day limits. All are category C islands except Lizard Island. See Cairns DCPW for permits and more information.

ACCESS
Australian Regional has flights running from Cairns for $115.

Contact:
Australian Regional
62 Abbott Street
Cairns
Queensland 4870
070 527700

See the next section, 'Beyond Lizard Island' for information about cruise boats that visit Lizard Island.

ACCOMMODATION
The resort on Lizard Island was built in 1975 by a consortium including Air Queensland (now Australian Regional). Sixty-four guests stay in bungalow accommodation facing a small, sandy beach. No children under six are allowed, and there are no TVs or air conditioners.

Suites cost $2100 per person per week with two adults sharing, and the Deluxe Suites cost $2450.

For bookings for Lizard Island Lodge, ring 070 503766 or 03 6663412.

CAMPING

The campground, at the northern end of **Watsons Beach**, has 25 spaces with tables, toilets, fireplaces and a pump for water. There is a limit of 14 days.

Campers are advised to walk from the airport to the campground because transport is expensive. Fuel is not permitted on the aircraft and provisions are not available from the resort.

WALKING TRACKS

The walk up to **Cooks Look** is steep and difficult, but is well worth it. It's so named because it's from here that Captain Cook tried to spot a way out to open sea through the Outer Reef. Cook named the island after seeing monitor lizards there.

Cooks Look is nearly 2 km from the campground.

There are other tracks marked on the map. The track to **Coconut Beach** is another difficult one.

CLOSEST DCPW OFFICE

Northern Regional Office
41 The Esplanade

PO Box 2066
Cairns
Queensland 4870
070 519811

NEAREST HELP
Royal Flying Doctor facilities and radio contact at the resort.

The main beach on Green Island.

Beyond Lizard Island

The islands off the Queensland coast north of Lizard Island are generally not the little paradises in the tropics that one might expect.

Battered by south-east Trade winds for much of the year, many of the islands tend to be windswept, barren, flat and rocky or mangrove cays. As well, they are isolated and difficult to get to. It is possible to gain access to the coast by tracks through some of the station properties but permission is needed from them first. Cruise boats call in to some islands but generally private boats are the only means of access.

Most people go there for what's in or under the water, not what's above it. Campers adventurous enough to come this far are advised to carry their own VHF radio, water, first-aid kit and copy of *Cruising the Coral Coast*.

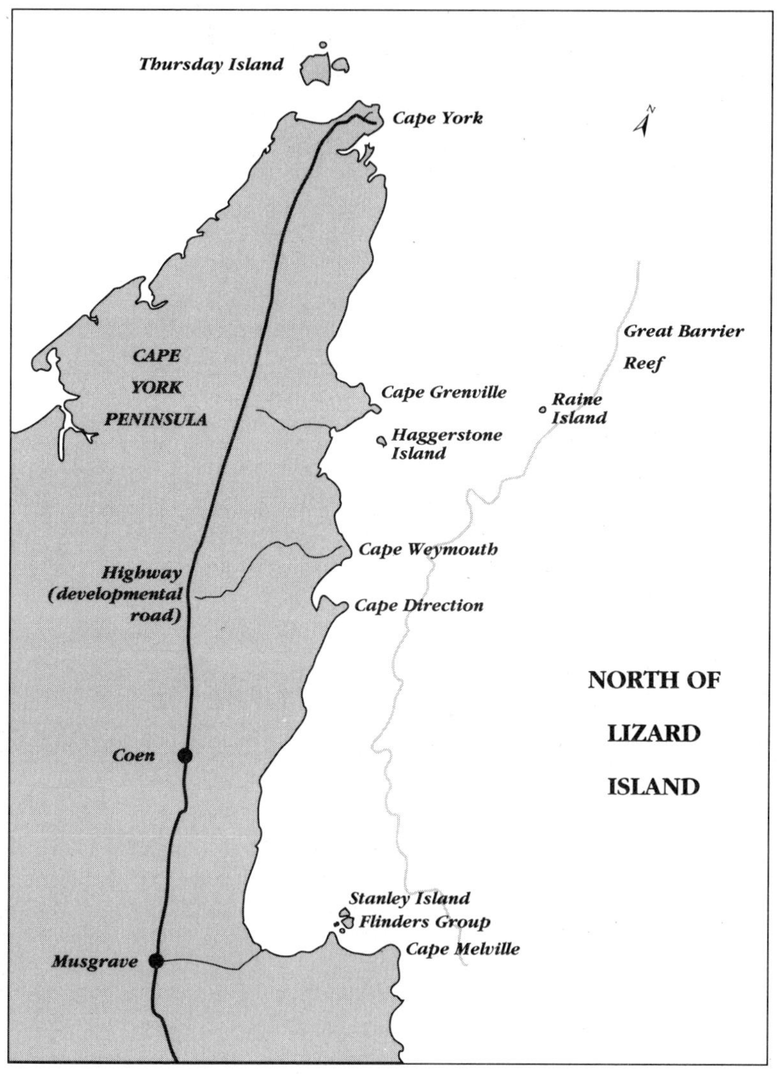
Thursday Island
Cape York
Great Barrier
Reef
CAPE
YORK
PENINSULA
Cape Grenville
Raine
Island
Haggerstone
Island
Cape Weymouth
Highway
(developmental
road)
Cape Direction
NORTH OF
LIZARD
ISLAND
Coen
Stanley Island
Flinders Group
Cape Melville
Musgrave

The Flinders Group

The **Flinders Group** are national park islands north of Lizard Island. Camping is permitted on all of them. They have category C status. The only residents on these islands are a few goats. The Owen Channel, which runs between Flinders and Stanley Islands, is a popular anchorage for trawlers.

The larger islands, such as Flinders, are covered in eucalypt woodland, and the smaller ones in mangroves. There is only seasonal water, except for two wells on a beach just south of the western tip of Flinders Island. More national parks were gazetted for islands north of the Flinders Group in early 1989.

Haggerstone, Raine and Thursday Islands

Haggerstone Island, off Cape Grenville, is a privately owned continental island sitting on a large coral reef.

Raine Island, on the Outer Reef, is a coral cay with prolific birdlife and is an important breeding ground for green turtles. The island is used by scientists as a reference site — its derelict beacon was built with convict labour in 1844. It has restricted access and a permit is needed from the DCPW for any landing.

The only other island that gets many visitors is **Thursday Island**, off the tip of Cape York. Once a romantic and major port for the pearling industry, it is now the administration and overpriced shopping centre of the **Torres Strait Islands**.

The Torres Strait Islands are perhaps better known these days following the release of the book *Castaway* dealing with the exploits of two Robinson Crusoes, one young and female, the other aging and male, on **Tuin Island**, near **Badu Island**. The book should be required reading for anyone contemplating such an experience.

ACCESS

Because of the strong winds and big tides common to the Torres Strait, small boats are not recommended. There are air services from Thursday Island (actually Horn Island, near Thursday) to other islands in the Torres Strait. Ring Sunbird Airlines in Cairns or on Thursday Island, 070 534544 or 070 691353.

There is a ferry service from Bamaga, a Torres Strait Islander settlement at the top of Cape York, to Thursday Island. Ring the operator in Bamaga on 070 691551. It costs $45 return.

Thursday Island is serviced by cruise boats and a trawler supply vessel from Cairns. These boats call in to other islands as well.

The *Queen of the Isles* is a comfortable passenger boat. It leaves from the main wharf in Cairns on Sundays at 8 p.m. and returns on the following Saturday morning. The three-day trip to Thursday Island visits Snapper, Hope and Lizard Islands. Other island visits for drop-offs are negotiable. Fares for the whole trip range from $550 for economy berths to $1150 for double state rooms. Ring 070 311844 or 008 079060 for details.

The *Noel Buxton* passenger boat is smaller and less comfortable than the *Queen of the Isles*. It has two and four-berth rooms ranging from $500 to $760. It leaves for Thursday Island from Shed 3 on the Cairns main wharf on Mondays at 8 p.m. and returns Sunday mornings. Ring Cape York Relaxa Cruises on 07 2637790.

The *Tropical Trader* is a mother ship for the trawler fleet that fishes up the coast to Thursday Island. It goes to any islands that have trawlers but regularly services Lizard and Haggerstone Islands and uses the Flinders Island anchorage. The *Tropical Trader* can take up to six passengers, either as workers on the boat for free or as paying passengers for $650 return. It takes ten days to do the 1000-nautical-mile trip. It leaves from Shed 5 on the main wharf. Ring 070 511470 for more information.

The *Atlantic Clipper* does the trip up to Thursday Island and visits Lizard Island. Telephone 070 312516 for details.

Trawler boat operators can often be found at the Barrier Reef Hotel opposite the main wharf for those interested in work on the boats. Make sure you've got a beer in hand.

Appendices

1. Mainland Backpackers and Youth Hostels

Queensland is going through a boom period in budget accommodation. Backpackers hostels are popping up everywhere. The traditional Youth Hostels, member hostels of Youth Hostels of Australia (YHA), are losing business to the independent Backpackers.

Youth Hostels have been criticized for having too many rules and regulations. They vary from hostel to hostel but some ban music and alcohol, insist on daily chores and the use of sleeping sheets and impose a lights-out curfew at 11p.m., or even 10 p.m .

Backpackers hostels vary greatly too. Some have no rules at all, while others, such as Backpackers by the Bay at Airlie Beach, have so many that they're run more like Youth Hostels.

It really comes down to what you want. If you're catching a boat to an island at 7 a.m., head for a YHA —.at least you can be sure of a good night's sleep. If you want to party all night, then Backpackers are probably more for you— but not all of them.

Because Backpackers hostels don't have a single governing body, as do the Youth Hostels, they vary dramatically in quality. There have been some moves to form umbrella organizations to represent the different hostels, but these are mainly for advertising purposes, not for reasons of maintaining standards.

Michael Higginson, who opened the first Backpacker hostel — the Backpacker Inn in Cairns — and is said to have actually coined the term, heads an organization called Aussie Backpackers. They put out the glossy *Backpacker Travel Magazine* and have formed the Backpackers Travel Company. Hostel Resorts of Australia publish the *Budget Accommodation and Travel Guide* and the poor-quality *Backpackers' News* newssheet. Another newssheet is put out by Backpackers Resorts of Australia from New South Wales.

The following is a list of hostels along the Queensland coast. Expect to pay between $6 and $10 for Youth Hostels and $8 and $12 for Backpackers.

YOUTH HOSTELS

At the time of writing there were YHAs at the Gold Coast, Brisbane and Woody Point (on the coast north of Brisbane), North Stradbroke Island, the Sunshine Coast, Hervey Bay, Rockhampton, Great Keppel Island, Mackay, Magnetic Island, Mission Beach, Cairns (at the old Belleview Motel on the Esplanade) and Cape Tribulation (Croodylus Village).

For membership and a guidebook to YHAs throughout Australia see the Head Office in Brisbane:

YHAQ
462 Queen Street
Brisbane
Queensland 4000
07 8312022

GPO Box 1128
Brisbane
Queensland 4001

BACKPACKERS HOSTELS

It's best to obtain lists of Backpackers hostels from the hostels themselves or by writing to:

Backpackers Resorts of Australia
3 Newman Street
Nambucca Heads NSW 2448

Enclose a stamped, self-addressed envelope.

Alternatively write (sending $5) to:
Hostel Resorts of Australia
11 Cook Road
Arcadia
Magnetic Island
Queensland 4819

Things change quickly in the budget accommodation industry so word of mouth is always best.

2. Buses and Trains

Buses and trains are the favoured means of transport for those travelling on a budget. Most prefer buses because they are more flexible and quieter. A train takes 34 hours to reach Cairns from Brisbane (it takes 29 hours to fly to Europe!), whereas buses can do it in 25 hours.

All the buslines stop at the major jumping off points to Queensland islands — Rockhampton, Mackay and Townsville — but not all services stop at Yeppoon (for Great Keppel), Shute Harbour (for the Whitsundays) or Mission Beach (for Dunk and the Family Islands). See details below.

A 20 percent discount is available to all students, pensioners and children.

All services begin at the Brisbane Transit Centre.

BUSES

McCaffertys has been operating in Queensland for 50 years. Three daily services run between Brisbane and Cairns, three run between Brisbane and Townsville, four between Brisbane and

Rockhampton and four between Brisbane and Bundaberg. They go to Airlie Beach and Shute Harbour but not to Yeppoon.

Fare: Brisbane/Cairns $97
Brisbane 07 2218555
Rockhampton 079 272844
Townsville 077 725100
Cairns 070 515899

Sunliner Express has three daily services between Brisbane and Cairns. Two go to Airlie Beach but not directly to Yeppoon.

Fare: Brisbane/Cairns $99
Brisbane 07 2296155
Townsville 077 726377
Cairns 070 513444

Deluxe has three daily services between Brisbane and Cairns and four from Brisbane to Townsville. Half of these services have connections with Yeppoon. All go to Airlie Beach and Shute Harbour.

Fare: Brisbane/Cairns $105
Brisbane 07 8442466
Townsville 077 726544
Cairns 070 312600

Greyhound has three daily services between Brisbane and Cairns — one is a double-deck coach with video for $105, one is a luxury coach for $105 and one is a regular coach.

Greyhound also has three daily services between Brisbane and Townsville. The regular bus and the double-deck service stop at Airlie Beach and Shute Harbour. No service to Yeppoon.

Brisbane 07 8443300
Rockhampton 079 225811
Townsville 077 712134
Cairns 070 513388

Ansett-Pioneer has three daily services between Brisbane and Cairns and three between Townsville and Cairns.

Fare: Brisbane/Cairns $105
Brisbane - Enquiries 07 8409393
- Reservations 07 8463633

TRAINS
The Sunlander leaves Brisbane for Cairns, and Cairns for Brisbane, every day, except Sunday, at 7.15 a.m.

Fares: Economy $100, First class $150.

The Queenslander leaves Brisbane on Sundays at 8.15 a.m. and Cairns on Tuesdays at 8.15 a.m.

Fares: Economy $100, First $287 (includes sleeping berth and meals)

The Capricornian operates between Brisbane and Rockhampton every day except Saturday.

Fares: Economy $51.40, First Class $81.80.
Reservations can be made at Central Reservations Bureau in Brisbane (07 2352222), Cairns (070 511218) or at many country and suburban railway stations.

There are discounts for students, pensioners and children. The Sunshine Rail Pass allows unlimited travel for 2, 3 or 4 weeks.

3. Maps

Sunmap tourist maps are well produced and adequate for locating the position of islands. There are maps that cover south-east, central and northern Queensland, one for the entire state and one covering the coast between Cairns and Cooktown. For more detailed maps see a Sunmap Centre for topographic maps in the 1:250,000 and 1:100,000 series.

Sunmap Centres Brisbane:	Anzac Square Adelaide Street Brisbane Queensland 4000 07 2276892 or write to: PO Box 40 Woollongabba Queensland 4102
Maryborough:	75 Lennox Street Maryborough Queensland 4065 071 221577
Bundaberg:	State Government Offices Quay Street Bundaberg Queensland 4670 071 738120
Rockhampton:	Trustee House 67 East Street Rockhampton Queensland 470 079 277582

Mackay:
50 Macalister Street
Mackay Queensland 474.
079 573506

Townsville:
State Government Offices
Cnr. Walker and Stanley Streets
Townsville Queensland 4810
077 221200

Cairns:
State Government Offices
36 Shields Street
Cairns Queensland 4870
070 523221

4. Working on the Islands

Working conditions vary enormously between islands. For example, a kitchenhand on Daydream Island in the Whitsundays could expect around $220 a week, with tax and rent/food costs taken out. Employees wre allowed to use all facilities open to guests, except the sauna and spa, and didn't have to pay for beach sports.

On Hamilton Island, also in the Whitsundays and the biggest employer of any of the islands, a housekeeper can expect about $270 a week, without tax, rent (about $25 a week) and meal costs taken out. There are no cooking facilities so staff must use the canteen. There is also an $80 deposit for a uniform. Employees cannot use the resort beach and travel 4 km to another beach.

Hamilton Island prefers people not to write but to appear in person for an interview. It's possible to get the Shute Harbour barge early in the morning for no cost.

Employment prospects constantly change, but tradespeople are often most in demand. Ring the personnel officers at the resorts and arrange to meet with them.

5. Great Barrier Reef Marine Park (GBRMP)

The GBRMP stretches from the bottom of the reef, near Bundaberg, to the tip of Cape York. The whole reef has World Heritage listing. The GBRMP is the result of the 'Save the Reef' campaign, and the end of oil drilling in the early 1970s.

The park is divided into four major sections: Mackay to Capricorn in the south, Townsville to Whitsunday, Cairns and Far Northern. The sections have been proclaimed progressively since 1979.

Each section is divided up into zones with different uses. These range from total protection in the Marine National Park B zones, to almost unrestricted use in the General Use A zones. Spearfishing is permitted only in General Use zones, and then only with snorkel and conventional speargun.

Zoning plans and activity guides are available from the Great Barrier Reef Marine Park Authority, PO Box 1379, Townsville Queensland 4810, 077 818811 or DCPW regional offices.

6. Division of Conservation, Parks and Wildlife (DCPW)

The DCPW is responsible for all national parks in the state, as well as for the-day-to day management of the GBRMP.

They regulate the numbers of campers and length of stay at each national park by issuing permits. Permits can be obtained for a fee from the local DCPW offices listed throughout the book. The offices have a list of rules and guidelines for campers, such as the need to take out all rubbish with you.

The DCPW head office is at 160 Ann Street, Brisbane, PO Box 155, North Quay Queensland 4002, 07 2278185.

7. Plants and Animals to Avoid

IN THE SEA

Marine stingers. Of the several varieties of stingers in Queensland waters — the Portuguese man-of-war or bluebottle (*Physalia*), the snottie or giant blubber (*Cyanea*), the little mauve stinger (*Pelagia*) and the varieties of *Carybdeid medusae* — the box jellyfish (*Chironex*) is the only one able to cause death in humans.

It is most common in shallow waters north of the Tropic of Capricorn between October and April, particularly near river and creek outflows into the sea after local rain. It is usually absent in rough seas, deep water and above coral.

In emergencies stay with the victim and give expired-air resuscitation if necessary. If possible, call for medical help. Flood the sting area with vinegar. Use a pressure immobilization technique (firm bandage and splint) if the sting is over a large area on a limb.

To get advice on emergency treatment, ring 008 079909 at any hour. Enquiries can be made with Australian Institute of Marine Science, at the James Cook University in Townsville (077 789211), Townsville Hospital (077 819211) or Cairns Hospital (070 506333).

Crocodiles. The much maligned saltwater crocodile (*Crocodylus porosus*) is a danger to humans along the Queensland coast. But the chances of getting skittled by a bus are a lot greater than of a saltwater croc making a meal of you.

The danger areas are the tidal reaches of rivers north of Rockhampton. But the crocodiles have been sighted along the coast and on some islands such as Hinchinbrook.

Some safety precautions are:

— swim only in areas of shallow rapids in rivers, not in deep water;

— keep away from the water's edge, particularly after dark;

— camp at least 50 m from the water's edge.

The smaller freshwater crocs (*Crocodylus johnstoni*) are not a threat to humans and it is safe to swim in areas where they are common.

Ciguatera poisoning is caused by eating some of the larger reef fish infected with toxic algae — particularly chinaman, red bass, paddletail and moray eels. Avoid all reef fish over 10 kg.

Poisoning causes tingling, numbness, itchiness, vomiting, cramps, diarrhoea or breathing difficulties.

Report poisonings to:
Southern Fisheries Research Centre
Department of Primary Industries
Deception Bay Queensland
07 2031444

Other marine nasties. Stonefish are small, spiky fish that inhabit shallow water. They can inflict bad wounds to feet if trodden on and are potentially fatal. Wear shoes in murky water. Vinegar or spirit on the wounds may relieve pain.

Toads, stingrays, cone shells and puffer-fish are to be avoided.

Oyster and coral cuts can easily get infected — see a doctor.

Shark attacks on humans are rare. There has never been one attack reported in the busiest group of islands, the Whitsundays.

'Tropical ear' is an infection caused by waterlogging — you should have been wearing ear plugs! See a doctor.

ON THE LAND

Stinging trees. Various species of the stinging tree, the *Dendrocnide* genus, inhabit the rainforests of Queensland. Their heart-shaped leaves and young branches are covered in fine hairs that break off into the skin on contact. The hairs contain an unknown poison which can cause a great deal of pain. Place sticking plaster on affected area and rip off quickly to get the hairs out of the skin. Antihistamines can be of value. Wear covering clothes when entering rainforests.

Leeches, common in damp areas such as rainforests, can be removed from the skin by covering them with salt or using the heat of a cigarette.

Snakes. Taipans, King browns, brown snakes and death adders are known to exist in Queensland. Firmly bandage and splint the limb and then go quickly to a hospital if you're unlucky enough to get bitten.

8. Further Reading

GENERAL

Cruising the Coral Coast, Alan Lucas, Horwitz Grahame, 1980 (a must for yachties).

Reader's Digest Guide to the Queensland Coast, Reader's Digest, 1986 (features the resort islands and some amazing aerial photography).

Australia — a Travel Survival Kit, Tony Wheeler, Lonely Planet, 1989.

National Parks of Queensland, Tony Groom, Cassell, 1980 (out of. print).

The Book of Australian Islands, Geoffrey Dutton, Macmillan, 1986

From the Dreaming to 1915 - A History of Queensland Ross Fitzgerald, University of Queensland Press, 1982.

From 1915 to the Early 1980s: A History of Queensland, Ross Fitzgerald, University of Queensland Press, 1984.

SPECIFIC

South Stradbroke Island, Lindy Salter, 1983.

Islands of Moreton Bay, Helen Horton, Boolarong Publications, 1983.

Discovering Fraser Island, John Sinclair, Pacific Maps.

Fraser Island: Sands of Time, Felicity Baverstock, ABC Books, 1985

Cruising the Curtis Coast, Noel Patrick, Riverstom Holding, 1986.

100 Magic Miles of the Great Barrier Reef, David Colfelt, Windward, 1985 (another one for the yachties).

Discovering Magnetic Island, James G. Porter, Kullari Publications, 1983.

Hinchinbrook Island, Arthur and Margaret Thorsborne, Weldon 1987.

Discovering the Family Islands, James G. Porter, Kullari Publications, 1983.

Cape York,, an Adventurer's Guide, Ron and Viv Moon, Kakirra, 1986.

Index

Islands with Resorts

Camping Islands with Facilities

Camping Islands without Facilities